Spring
Wild Flowers
of
West
Virginia

Spring
Wild Flowers
of West
Virginia

EARL L. CORE

Illustrations by William A. Lunk

WEST VIRGINIA UNIVERSITY PRESS

MORGANTOWN 2005

Spring Wild Flowers

ISBN (paperback) 0-937058-95-5 (alk. paper)

Library of Congress Cataloguing-in-Publication Data

Core, Earl Lemley, 1902-1984
Spring wild flowers of West Virginia
Third Edition; illustrations by William A. Lunk.
vii, 104 p. : ill. ; 22 cm.
1. Wild flowers–West Virginia–Identification. 2. Plants–Identification. I. title. II. Core, Earl
Lemley. III. Lunk, William A.

Cover Design by Than Saffel

Foreword

Wild flowers constitute a most substantial portion of that delightful ensemble we call spring. With the ever-increasing industrialization and urbanization of our people the need for recreation in the restful peace and quiet of the wilderness becomes increasingly urgent, and it is in the spring especially that folks, weary of the routine of winter, turn to nature for psychological and physiological relief. But wilderness areas in West Virginia are not nearly as extensive as they once were and the need for conservation of those we still have cannot be over-emphasized.

The natural conditions which favor the growth of our favorite spring wild flowers are, happily, those which favor the development of the wilderness as a whole—its trees, its animals, its soil, its water supply.

To the nature lover this treatise is offered with the hope that it may be helpful in providing information concerning our spring wild flowers and stimulate new efforts to maintain habitats in which they may be enjoyed.

> *"One impulse from a vernal wood*
> *May teach you more of man,*
> *Of moral evil and of good,*
> *Than all the sages can."*
>
> —WORDSWORTH

Introduction

The first edition of this book appeared in 1948 and it has gone through several printings. Much research on the subject has transpired since that time and it is a pleasure to acknowledge contributions made by former students, colleagues, and others, too numerous to enumerate.

Nearly 250 species of spring wild flowers found in West Virginia are described herein. Common or English names and scientific or Latin names are given for each species. The descriptions are in two sections, the first a popular account giving such information as meaning of the names, uses, habitats, ranges in West Virginia, etc., followed by a more detailed description of the plant itself.

In this account, descriptions are given of the stems, leaves, flowers, sepals, petals, stamens, and pistils in the order named. Flowering dates are given. For ease of consultation, the plates giving illustrations of the species appear on pages facing the descriptions.

In checking the identification of a flower, both the sketches and the descriptions should be carefully compared with the specimen being studied. No keys are given but an index is provided for ready reference. The terms used are mostly simple and easily understood. More difficult ones are usually explained in the text. No glossary is provided but definitions for all terms used can be found in a good dictionary.

The Author

Earl L. Core, professor emeritus of biology at West Virginia University, also is co-author of the four-volume *Flora of West Virginia*. The University's 75-acre Core Arboretum was named for him. He received his bachelor's and master's degrees from West Virginia University and his doctorate from Columbia University.

Spring
Wild Flowers
of
West
Virginia

Golden Club
Orontium aquaticum L.

Common in shallow streams, ponds and swamps, particularly in the eastern part of the State, the Golden Club is interesting mainly as an oddity because of the dark green leaves and the curious slender yellow "club" or *spadix* over which the small flowers are compactly clustered. It is related to the jack-in-the-pulpit and the skunk cabbage, but the spathe is very small.—Leaves long-stalked, oblong, often floating. Flowers small and inconspicuous, yellowish. April-May.

Jack-in-the-Pulpit. Indian Turnip
Arisaema triphyllum (L.) Schott.

These quaint little preachers, almost hidden in their delicate striped pulpits, are well known in every county of the State, growing in rich woods. They are desirable for the wild flower garden and easily transplanted. Autumn is the best time for removal. The bulb-like base or *corm* ("turnip") is intensely acrid, but is highly nutritious and loses its acridity upon cooking. It was highly prized by the Indians. A favorite school-boy trick was tempting others to bite into the blistering corm.—Leaves generally two, each divided into three leaflets. Flowers small and inconspicuous, packed about the lower part of the spadix ("jack"). Spathe ("pulpit") pale green or dark purple, variegated with spots or stripes. April-June.

Calamus
Acorus calamus L.

Throughout the State, in swamps and along the margins of small streams, the slender Calamus (or Sweet Flag) is a familiar plant. Early settlers collected the aromatic rootstocks (rhizomes) to dry them for reputed medicinal value and farm boys learned to chew them.—Leaves green, ribbon-like, the upper one a sort of continuation of the flower stalk, acting as a spathe. Flowers small, on a spadix. May-July.

Skunk Cabbage
Symplocarpus foetidus (L.) Nutt.

Aside from such "ever-blooming" plants as the common chickweed, the Skunk Cabbage possesses the honor of being our earliest spring flower, since it is often found in swampy or boggy ground as early as February. Unfortunately, it has an odor so unpleasant as to win for itself a most unromantic name. This odor, however, attracts large numbers of small flies and other insects, by means of which the flowers are pollinated. Throughout the State.—Leaves large, appearing later than the flowers and becoming one or two feet long. Flowers small and inconspicuous, packed on a globular spadix. Spathe spotted and striped with yellowish-green and purple. February-April.

Green Dragon
Arisaema dracontium (L.) Schott.

The Green Dragon somewhat resembles the Indian turnip but bears only one compound leaf, with more than three leaflets, while the spadix, instead of being hidden in the spathe, projects far beyond into a long slender point. It is found in rich low, usually shady ground in most parts of the State, but much less common than the preceding.—Leaf single, compound, of 5 to 17 leaflets. Flowers small and inconspicuous, dull greenish-white, clustered at the base of the spadix. Spathe oblong, twisted, pointed, greenish. May-June.

2

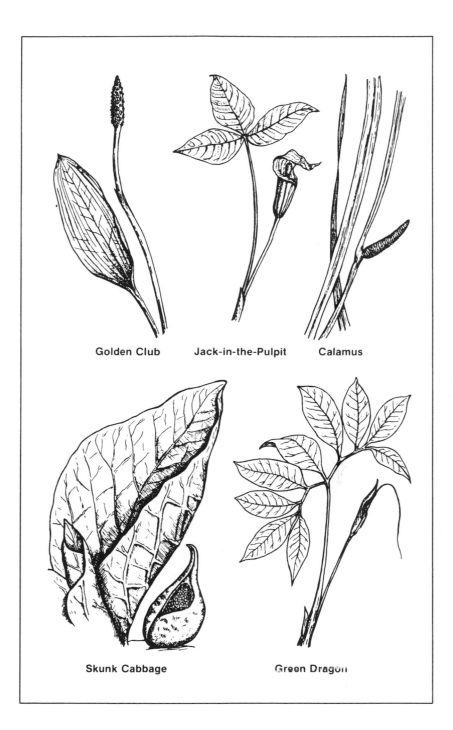

Golden Club   Jack-in-the-Pulpit   Calamus

Skunk Cabbage   Green Dragon

3

Yellow Fawn Lily. Yellow Adder's Tongue
Erythronium americanum Ket.

In rich moist woods where the pale sunshine of early April filters through the leafless branches of the trees we often find the ground thickly dotted with hundreds of these beautiful yellow lilies, each arising between a pair of mottled erect leaves, from deep solid scaly corms. Found throughout the State.—Leaves elliptical, mottled with purplish or whitish blotches. Flowers nodding, light yellow. Perianth of 6 recurved divisions, 1-1½ inches long, the three innermost auricled at base. Stamens 6. Pistil 1. March-May.

Umbilicate Fawn Lily
Erythronium umbilicatum Parks & Hardin

The Umbilicate Fawn Lily is found in rich woods, mostly in the eastern counties, from Hampshire to Summers. Umbilicate means "like a navel" and refers to the indentation at the tip of the capsule.—Leaves elliptical, mottled. Flowers yellow. Perianth divisions not auricled. Stamens 6. Pistil 1. March-May.

White Fawn Lily. White Adder's Tongue
Erythronium albidum Nutt.

This species is quite similar to those above, except that it bears a white flower and produces narrower leaves with fewer spots or sometimes without spots. It also arises from a deep corm. It is not nearly as common in West Virginia and is mainly found in the western counties.—Leaves elliptical. Flowers pinkish-white. Perianth of 6 divisions. Stamens 6. Pistil 1. March-May.

Blazing Star
Chamaelirium luteum (L.) Gray

The Blazing Star, found in wet meadows locally throughout the State, grows from one to four feet high, its straight slender stem bearing a close raceme of small but attractive white flowers. The staminate and pistillate flowers appear on different plants.—Leaves flat, the lower ones spatulate, in a rosette near the ground, the others smaller, scattered alternately along the stem. Flowers fragrant. Perianth of six segments. Stamens 6 (in the staminate flowers). Pistil 1 (in the pistillate flowers). May-July.

Wild Garlic
Allium canadense L.

In late spring the pretty flowers of the wild garlic appear in rich moist meadows where it is often eaten by cattle and leads to the production of onion-scented milk. The flowering stalk arising from a coated bulb resembling the garden onion, is usually only about 1 to 1½ feet high, with the long linear leaves mostly near the base. Common throughout the State.—Flowers pink or white, in umbels, often replaced by small bulbets ("onion sets"). Perianth of 6 distinct uniformly colored parts. Stamens 6. Pistil 1. May-June.

Spiderwort
Tradescantia virginiana L.

In moist rich soil, generally along streams, the Common Spiderwort is mostly found in the eastern counties. The rich blue or purple flowers are very handsome, but quite perishable and last only a few hours. The stem gives off a sticky juice which spins into threads, giving rise to the common name.—Stems leafy, erect, ½ to 3 feet tall. Leaves linear, somewhat hairy. Flowers clustered, 1 to 2 inches wide. Sepals 3, green. Petals 3, blue or purple. Stamens 6, with hairy filaments. Pistil 1. May-August.

4

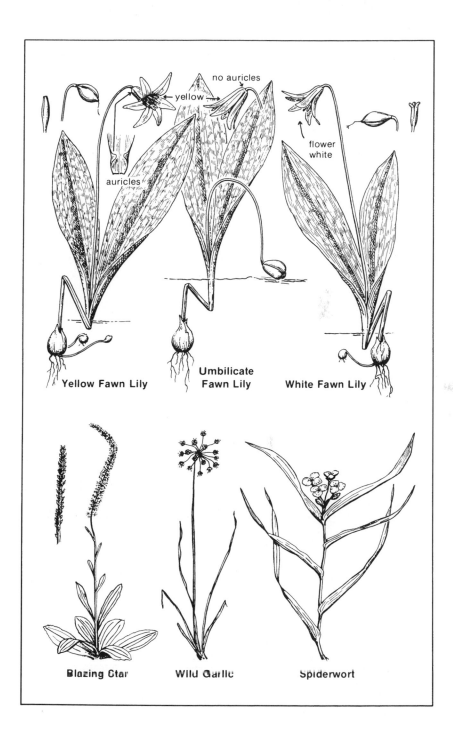

no auricles

yellow →

auricles

flower
white

Yellow Fawn Lily

**Umbilicate
Fawn Lily**

White Fawn Lily

Blazing Star

Wild Garlic

Spiderwort

5

Mountain Bellwort
Uvularia pudica (Walt.) Fernald.

This species has a curious distribution, being found both in pine-barrens along the Atlantic coast and in mountain woods in the Appalachians. In West Virginia it occurs most frequently in the southern counties. It differs from the preceding species principally in having the leaves rounded at the base.—Stems sparingly rough-pubescent, at least at the forks. Leaves sessile, bright green on both sides, the base rounded. Flowers 1 or 2, an inch long, pale yellow, drooping. Perianth of 6 divisions. Stamens 6. Pistil 1, the style 3-parted. May-June.

Sessileleaf Bellwort
Uvularia sessilifolia (L.) Wats.

A very pretty but modest little plant, this species is locally common throughout the State in open dry woods. It differs from the two preceding species in that its leaves are sessile but not perfoliate.—Stems glabrous, angled, curving. Leaves glaucous below, lance-oblong, pointed at each end, sessile. Flowers one or two, drooping, bell-shaped, ½ to 1 inch long. Perianth of 6 pale yellow divisions. Stamens 6. Pistil 1, with a 3-parted style. May-June.

Large-Flowered Bellwort
Uvularia grandiflora Sm.

The graceful stems and nodding lemon-yellow flowers of this Bellwort appear in rich moist woods, probably in every county in the State. It is the largest of the Bellworts, about 24 inches high. The leaves seem to be penetrated near the base by the stem. The lily-like flowers average nearly two inches in length. The "wort," which appears as the common name of many plants, is an Old English word meaning plant or herb.— Stem not glaucous, forked above the middle, usually with one leaf below the fork. Leaves oblong, perfoliate, downy beneath. Flowers one or two on each plant. Perianth of 6 uniform, pale yellow divisions. Stamens 6. Pistil 1, the style 3-parted. April-June.

Mealy Bellwort
Uvularia perfoliata L.

Very near of kin to the last, this Bellwort also has leaves seemingly pierced by the stem ("perfoliate"), but is in general a somewhat smaller plant, about 8 to 20 inches high. It is found throughout the State in very much the same habitats, in moist woods.—Stem glaucous, forked, with 1, 2, or 3 leaves below the fork. Leaves oblong, perfoliate, not downy beneath. Flowers bell-shaped, about 1 inch long, hanging on a slender stalk, like the *uvula*, or soft palate, whence the generic name. Perianth of 6 pale yellow divisions, mealy on the inner face. Stamens 6. Pistil 1, the style 3-parted.

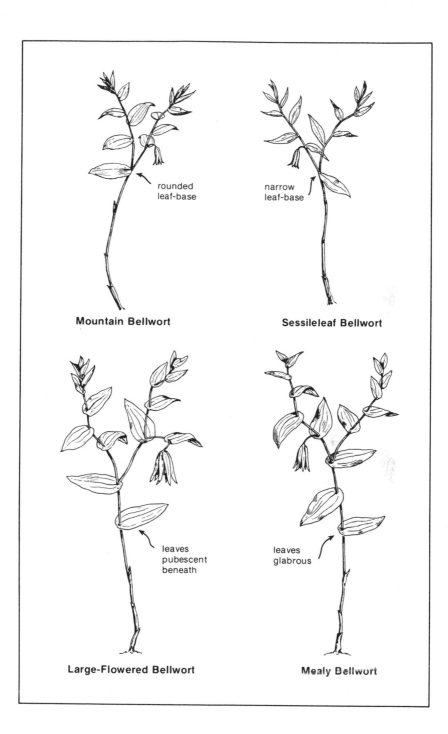

rounded
leaf-base

narrow
leaf-base

Mountain Bellwort

Sessileleaf Bellwort

leaves
pubescent
beneath

leaves
glabrous

Large-Flowered Bellwort

Mealy Bellwort

Star-of-Bethlehem
Ornithogalum umbellatum L.

This is a beautiful little plant which was introduced from Europe as an ornamental and has become quite well established in lawns, fields, and roadsides as an escape. The leaves and flower stalk arise in clusters from a coated bulb.—Scape 4-10 inches high. Leaves linear. Flowers upright, 5 to 8, on long stalks. Perianth divisions 6, white, with a green line in the middle on the under side. Stamens 6. Pistil 1. May-June.

Mandarin
Disporum maculatum (Buckl.) Britton

This species is very similar to the above but in West Virginia is known only from the southernmost counties (McDowell and Mingo). It differs in having the perianth spotted ("maculate") with purple.—Leaves sessile, ovate. Flowers 1½-2½ cm. long. Perianth bell-shaped. Stamens 6. Pistil 1. Fruit yellow. April-May.

Disporum
Disporum lanuginosum (Michx.) Nichols

A graceful plant of rich woods, this species is probably found in every county of the State. It is somewhat hairy throughout, sparingly branched with flowers mostly solitary at the ends of the branches. The name Disporum ("two-seeds") refers to the fact that there are generally two seeds in each cavity of the fruit.—Stems arising from creeping rootstocks. Leaves sessile, ovate. Flowers ½ to 1 inch long, greenish-yellow. Perianth bell-shaped, of 6 uniform divisions. Stamens 6. Pistil 1, stigmas 3. Fruit red. May-June.

Canada Mayflower
Maianthemum canadense Desf.

In rich moist woods these little plants sometimes grow in such profusion as to nearly cover over a considerable area with their deep green leaves and lacy white flowers. It is our only lily with 4-parted flowers.—Stem 3 to 6 inches high, with 2 or 3 leaves. Leaves oval, heart-shaped. Flowers white, in a raceme. Perianth of 4 divisions. Stamens 4. Pistil one, stigma 2-lobed. May-July.

Yellow Clintonia
Clintonia borealis (Ait.) Raf.

In moist cool woods of the mountain counties our attention is attracted by the large, rich green, shining leaves of this lovely plant. The flowers are produced on a scape which is sheathed at the base by two, three, or four leaves. Named for DeWitt Clinton, governor of New York and builder of the Erie Canal.—Scape 6 to 16 inches high, from a slender rootstock. Leaves oblong, conspicuous. Flowers 3 to 6, greenish-yellow, about a half inch long. Perianth of 6 uniform divisions. Stamens 6. Pistil 1. May-June.

White Clintonia
Clintonia umbellulata (Michx.) Morong.

The White Clintonia likewise occurs in moist woods but at lower elevations and is found, probably, in every county in the State. The leaves are generally broader and the plant as a whole is more beautiful than its near relative.—Scape 8 to 18 inches high. Leaves ciliate. Flowers 12 to 30, white, sometimes dotted with purple or green, less than half an inch long. Perianth of 6 uniform divisions. Stamens 6. Pistil 1. May-June.

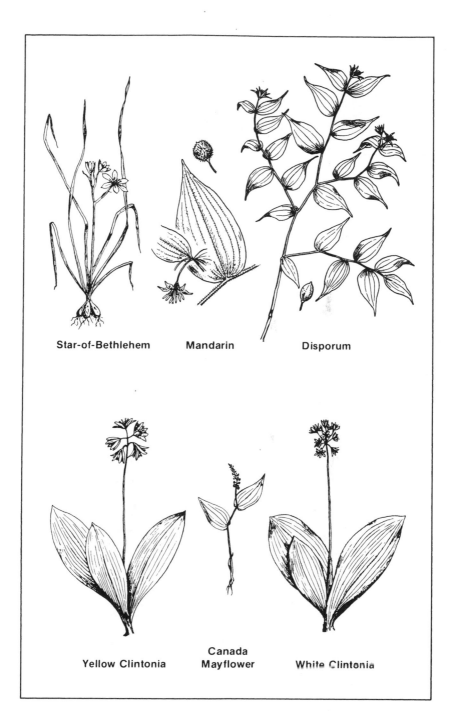

Star-of-Bethlehem   Mandarin   Disporum

Yellow Clintonia

Canada
Mayflower

White Clintonia

Twistedstalk
Streptopus roseus Michx.

The graceful forking branches and pointed leaves almost hide the pink, bell-shaped flowers of this denizen of cold damp mountain woods. The name refers to the slender flower stalks which are abruptly bent near the middle.—Stems 8 to 24 inches high, zigzag, forking. Leaves taper-pointed, sessile. Flowers rose-purple, hanging, generally in pairs, from the axils, less than a half-inch long. Perianth of 6 uniform divisions. Stamens 6. Pistil 1, with a 3-cleft stigma. May-June.

Plumelily. Wild Spikenard. False Solomon's Seal
Smilacina racemosa (L.) Desf.

Throughout the State, in rich, moist woods, the gracefully curved stem of the Plumelily is a familiar sight. Despite a general resemblance to the true Solomon's Seal, it is sufficiently different to deserve an individual name and the name Plumelily is suggested to replace the old awkward titles.—Stems 1 to 3 feet high. Leaves oval, 4 to 6 inches long. Flowers greenish-white, small, a large number together in a terminal panicle. Perianth of 6 uniform divisions. Stamens 6. Pistil 1. May.

Starflower Solomon's Seal
Smilacina stellata (L.) Desf.

This plant somewhat resembles the preceding but produces only a few flowers in an unbranched raceme. It occurs in moist soil of shady banks but is much less common than the last species, being found principally in the southern counties.—Stems 8 to 20 inches high, nearly glabrous. Leaves oblong-lanceolate, slightly clasping the stem. Flowers less than a quarter of an inch long, white. Perianth of 6 uniform divisions. Stamens 6. Pistil 1. May-June.

Mountain Lily-of-the-Valley
Convallaria montana Raf.

In rich woods of the high Alleghenies there may be found the American cousin of our garden lily-of-the-valley, which came to us from Europe. The native plant differs only slightly from the one so familiar in cultivation, but is regarded as a distinct species. It is quite rare in West Virginia.—Scape 4 to 10 inches tall, the base sheathed by 2 leaves tapering at both ends, 5 to 12 inches long. Flowers white, fragrant, nodding in a 1-sided raceme. Perianth of 6 uniform divisions, less than half an inch long. Stamens 6. Pistil 1. May-June.

Indian Cucumberroot
Medeola virginiana L.

Rich damp woods provide the proper habitat for this plant, and it probably grows in such situations in every county of West Virginia. The tuberous white rootstock has something of the flavor and shape of the cucumber and was used by the Indians as food and as a liver tonic. The generic name is from the sorceress Medea, on account of the supposed medicinal virtues of the plant.—Stem 1 to 3 feet high. Leaves in 2 whorls on flowering plants, the lower of 5 to 9 leaves, the upper of 3 or 4 smaller ones. Flowers small, greenish-yellow. Perianth of 3 sepals and 3 petals, uniform in color. Stamens 6, reddish-brown. Pistil 1, with 3 recurved, reddish-brown stigmas. May-June.

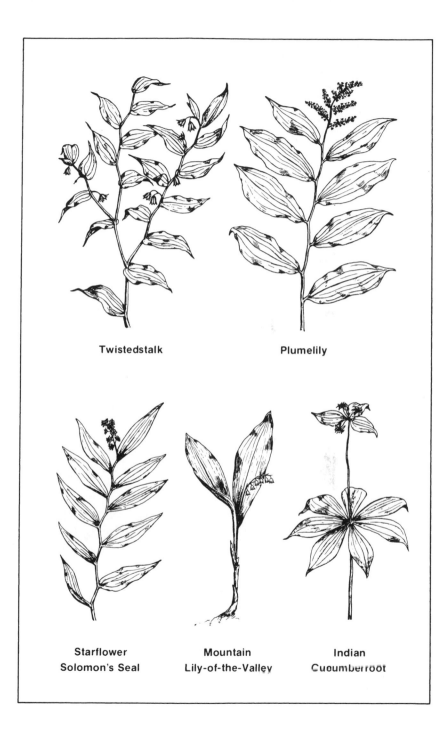

Twistedstalk

Plumelily

Starflower
Solomon's Seal

Mountain
Lily-of-the-Valley

Indian
Cucumberroot

Common Solomon's Seal
Polygonatum biflorum (Walt.) Ell.

The graceful curving stems of the Solomon's Seal are among the most decorative features of our spring woods and they doubtless occur in every county of the State. The common name was suggested by the large scars left on the rootstocks by the abscission of the flowering stalks of previous years, which somewhat resemble the impression of a seal upon wax.—Stem slender, curving, 1 to 2 feet high, bearing a leaf-like cauline bract. Leaves alternate, smooth beneath, oval, the mid-vein prominent for the full length. Flowers yellowish, bell-shaped, 1 or 2 nodding from most of the leaf axils. Perianth united, 6-lobed. Stamens 6. Pistil 1. April-June.

Downy Solomon's Seal
Polygonatum pubescens (Willd.) Pursh

In most of the counties of West Virginia, at least to the west of the Alleghenies, this closely related species may be found associated with the Common Solomon's Seal. It can easily be distinguished by the fact that the cauline bract is papery and falls early leaving a scar, whereas in the preceding species the bract is leaf-like and persistent.—Stems 1 to 1½ feet high, curving. Leaves oval, downy beneath. Flowers yellowish, usually 1 or 2 from most of the leaf axils. Perianth bell-shaped, 6-lobed. Stamens 6. Pistil 1. April-June.

Great Solomon's Seal
Polygonatum commutatum (Schultes f.) Dietr.

The largest of the three species of Solomon's Seal found in West Virginia grows in moist rich soil of meadows and shaded river banks, and blossoms somewhat later in the spring. All three species possess a much-jointed rootstock, to which the generic name, signifying *many* and *knee*, refers.—Stem 2 to 7 feet high, glabrous, stout, curving. Leaves oval, with numerous veins prominent for the full length. Flowers greenish-yellow, usually 3 or more from most of the leaf axils. Perianth bell-shaped, 6-lobed. Stamens 6. Pistil 1. May-June.

Stargrass. Colicroot
Aletris farinosa L.

This plant is found in dry sandy soil, chiefly in the central and southern counties. The dried rootstocks were used as crude drugs.—Scape 2 to 3 feet high. Leaves in a cluster at the base. Flowers white. Perianth 6-cleft. Stamens 6. Pistil 1. May-June.

Carrionflower
Smilax herbacea L.

Like "a dead rat in the wall" is Thoreau's characterization of the odor of the flowers of this otherwise handsome plant, common everywhere in West Virginia along riverbanks and in moist soil of meadows. It climbs by means of slender tendrils borne in pairs from the leaf axils.—Stems 3 to 15 feet high, herbaceous. Leaves ovate or rounded, usually heart-shaped at base. Flowers small, in umbels from the leaf axils, 20 to 40 in each umbel. Perianth greenish-yellow, of 6 uniform parts. Stamens 6. Pistil 1, with 3 spreading stigmas. The plants are dioecious, that is, the stamens and pistils occur in separate flowers on different plants. May-June.

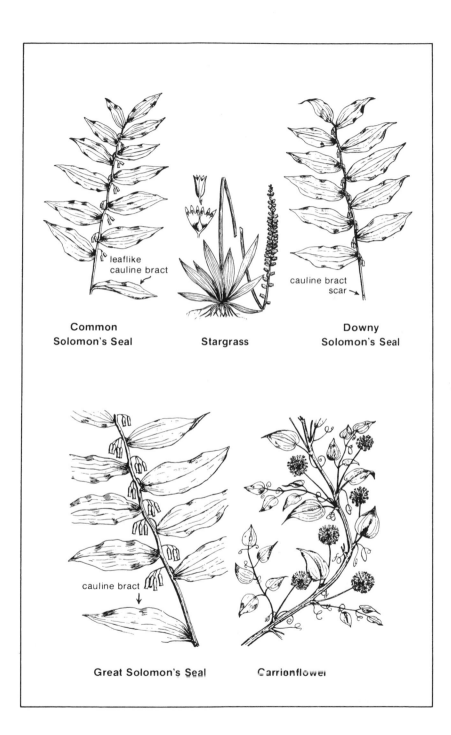

Common
Solomon's Seal

Stargrass

Downy
Solomon's Seal

leaflike
cauline bract

cauline bract
scar

cauline bract

Great Solomon's Seal

Carrionflower

Ill-Scented Trillium. Wake Robin
Trillium erectum L.

In moist rich woods in every county of the State the Wake Robin is a familiar wild flower. Harned compares its odor to that of carrion or a wet dog and Mrs. Dana agrees that it is most unpleasant. Nevertheless, the Wake Robin comprises for the most of us a part of that pleasant ensemble we call spring, because the season is already fully here when its flowers appear, despite the implication of earliness in the common name Wake Robin.—Stems stout, 1 to 1½ feet high, from a tuberous rootstock. Leaves broadly ovate, 3 in a whorl at the summit of the stem. Flower single, terminal. Calyx of 3 green sepals. Corolla of 3 petals, usually purplish-red, sometimes white, pink, green, or yellow. Stamens 6. Pistil 1, with 3 spreading stigmas. April-June.

Large-Flowered Trillium
Trillium grandiflorum (Michx.) Salisb.

The name Trillium is from the Latin word *tres,* three, in reference to the fact that the parts of the flower are arranged in threes. This is the largest and most beautiful of the Trilliums. Of all the spring wild flowers, none is more familiar nor more characteristic of rich woodlands throughout the State. Like white stars they gleam in deep woods in every county.—Stem 8 to 20 inches high. Leaves oval, 3 in a whorl. Flower single, terminal, showy. Calyx of 3 green sepals. Corolla of 3 white petals, turning pink in age. Stamens 6. Pistil 1, with 3 stigmas. April-May.

Sessile Trillium
Trillium sessile L.

The Sessile Trillium resembles the Ill-scented Trillium in color but it has no flower stalk and the flower is borne close to the bases of the leaves. Instead of being ill-scented, the flowers are slightly fragrant. It occurs with the other Trilliums in forested areas, probably in every county in the State.—Stem 4 to 8 inches high. Leaves usually blotched or mottled. Flowers single, terminal, sessile. Calyx of 3 green sepals. Corolla of 3 petals, dull reddish-purple, varying to greenish-yellow. Stamens 6. Pistil 1, of 3 stigmas.

Snowy Trillium
Trillum nivale Riddell

Cold, damp, mountain ravines provide the suitable habitat for this species, the earliest, smallest, and rarest of our Trilliums. Its small white flowers often appear before the March snows have melted away. It will survive transplanting to lower elevations and makes an attractive addition to the early wild flower garden.—Stem 2 to 6 inches high. Leaves oval, only 1 to 2 inches long. Flower single, terminal, stalked. Calyx of 3 green sepals. Corolla of 3 white petals. Stamens 6. Pistil 1, with 3 spreading stigmas. March-May.

Painted Trillium
Trillium undulatum Willd.

This pretty species is quite common in cold damp woods throughout the higher Alleghenies in the eastern part of the State. It is smaller and less showy than the Large-flowered Trillium, but to many people it is fully as attractive, with its white petals painted at the base with red stripes.—Stems 8 to 20 inches high. Leaves ovate, pointed. Flower single, terminal, stalked. Calyx of 3 green sepals. Corolla of 3 white petals, striped with crimson. Stamens 6. Pistil 1, with 3 stigmas.

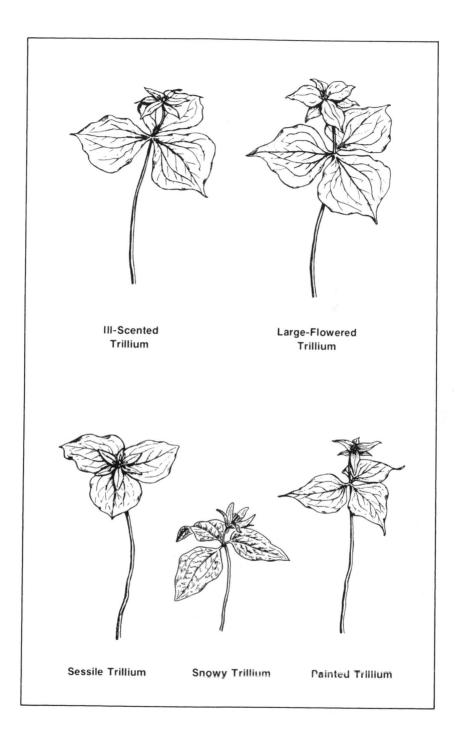

Ill-Scented
Trillium

Large-Flowered
Trillium

Sessile Trillium   Snowy Trillium   Painted Trillium

Wild Hyacinth
Camassia scillioides (Raf.) Cory

To find the pale blue racemes of the Wild Hyacinth is of sufficient rarity in West Virginia to make its discovery notable. It has been found occasionally in rich soil of low meadows and along streams in the counties of the central and southern part of the State. The flower stalk is virtually leafless, the linear leaves appearing about its base.—Scape 6-30 inches high, arising from a coated bulb. Leaves narrow. Flowers in an elongated raceme. Perianth of 6 uniform parts, pale blue or lilac, about half an inch long. Stamens 6. Pistil 1, style 1. April-May.

Mucronate Blue-eyedgrass
Sisyrinchium mucronatum Michx.

The Blue-eyedgrass, as indicated by the name, has grass-like leaves and flowers that peep out from among the meadow grasses like bright blue eyes. It is a perennial herb with fibrous roots. Of the two species found in West Virginia, this may be easily identified by its unbranched stem and purple-tinged spathes. It occurs locally throughout the State.—Stem 4-20 inches high, winged. Leaves grass-like, narrow. Flowers in umbels. Perianth segments 6, violet-blue, tipped with a mucro. Stamens 3. Pistil 1, style 3-cleft, stigmas 3. May-June.

Yellow Stargrass
Hypoxis hirsuta (L.) Coville

So closely do the leaves of this species resemble grass that the plant might easily be overlooked were it not for the pretty bright yellow flowers. The flowers and leaves arise separately from a small bulb. It is common in dry or sandy soil of meadows and open woods.—Scape 6 to 8 inches high, bearing 1 to 4 flowers. Leaves linear, grass-like, hairy. Flowers less than a half inch long. Perianth of 6 similar parts, the divisions greenish outside, hairy within. Stamens 6. Pistil 1, style 1. May-October.

Common Blue-eyedgrass
Sisyrinchium angustifolium Mill.

This is by far the commoner of the two species of Blue-eyedgrass in West Virginia, being found in abundance in wet or dry soil of grassy places in every county. It can be identified by its branched stem, the several spathes being borne on long pedicels.— Stems in clumps, 4-20 inches high, winged. Leaves grass-like. Spathes green. Flowers in umbels. Perianth parts 6, blue. Stamens 3. Pistil 1, style 3-parted, stigmas 3.

Dwarf Iris
Iris verna L.

On shaded hillsides and in woods of the mountain counties the Dwarf Iris is an occasional botanical prize, but it is usually not at all common. The name Iris is from the Greek, meaning rainbow, and is most appropriately applied to these plants, with violet-blue or white flowers, orange-yellow at the base.—Stems 2 to 6 inches high, arising from a creeping rootstock. Leaves grass-like, less than ⅜ of an inch wide. Flowers 1 to 3. Perianth of 3 sepals and 3 petals similarly colored, blue and yellow. Stamens 3. Pistil 1, stigmas 3, resembling petals. April-May.

Crested Iris
Iris cristata Ait.

The Crested Iris is somewhat larger than the preceding species, with broader leaves, and is much more common, being found in rich woods in all parts of West Virginia. The name refers to the elevated ridge or crest on the upper surface of each sepal.— Stems 2 to 6 inches high. Leaves about ½ to ¾ inches wide. Flowers blue, fragrant, usually solitary. Sepals 3, petal-like. Petals 3. Stamens 3. Pistil 1, stigmas 3, petal-like. April-May.

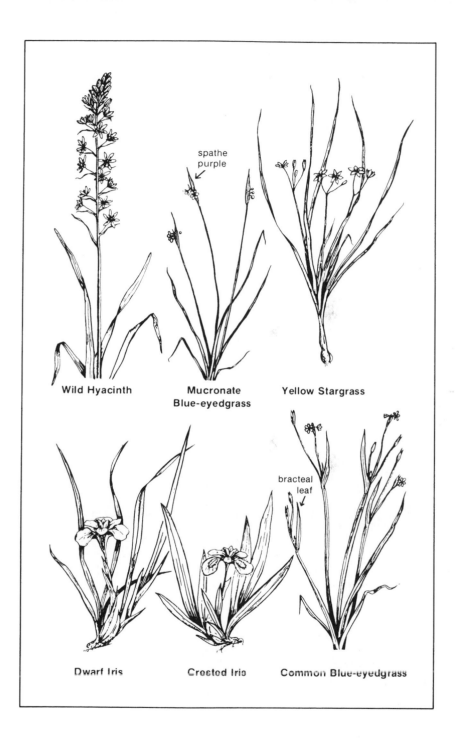

Wild Hyacinth

spathe purple

Mucronate
Blue-eyedgrass

Yellow Stargrass

Dwarf Iris

Crested Iris

bracteal leaf

Common Blue-eyedgrass

Beardflower. Adder's Mouth
Pogonia ophioglossoides (L.) Ker

This orchid is mostly a summer flower but may be found in bloom in sphagnum bogs in the mountain counties as early as late May.—Stem 6 to 9 inches high. A single leaf is borne near the middle of the stem. Flowers pink (rarely white), fragrant, 1 inch long. Lip bearded. May-August.

Whorled Pogonia
Isotria verticillata (Willd.) Raf.

This little orchid occurs in acid woods, often with mountain laurel and teaberry, more or less throughout the State, but seldom abundant.—Stem 8 to 12 inches high. Leaves in a terminal whorl of 5. Flowers greenish-yellow, less than 1 inch long. Lip crested. May-June.

Showy Orchis
Orchis spectabilis

The charming little Showy Orchis in most places is the first member of the Orchid family to appear in the spring. To discover it is somewhat of a pleasant surprise, for though it is generally distributed in rich woods over the State it is nowhere common. Its magenta-pink-and-white flowers are showy, but not large.—Scape 4 to 8 inches high, 4-angled, few-flowered. Leaves 2, oblong, shining, sheathing the scape at the base. Flowers in a loose raceme. Sepals 3. Petals 3, the middle one (the lip) white. Stamens and pistil grown together in a structure called the column. April-June.

Wister's Coralroot
Corallorhiza wisteriana Conrad

Rare indeed is an encounter with this dull brownish-purple or yellowish orchid, totally lacking in green color, living as a saprophyte in moist rich soil of deep woods. It is known in West Virginia only from Barbour, Pocahontas, Cabell, and Wayne counties, but it doubtless escapes attention in many places.—Stem 6 to 16 inches high, arising from a much-branched coral-like rootstock. Leaves developed merely as sheaths, not green. Flowers 12 to 16, in a loose raceme. Perianth less than half an inch long. Lip white with purple spots. March-May.

Adam-and-Eve. Puttyroot
Aplectrum hyemale (Muhl.) Torr.

The Puttyroot grows from a slender rootstock which every year produces a globe-shaped corm, somewhat soft like a lump of putty. Usually this year's and last year's corms are found joined together by the rootstock, whence the name Adam-and-Eve. Late in the summer the corm sends up a large oval leaf which lasts through the winter and in the next spring the flower stalk appears. It is found over the State in rich woods, but nowhere abundant.—Scape 12 to 18 inches high. Leaf solitary. Flowers about 10 in a loose raceme. Sepals 3, greenish or yellowish, tinged with purple. Petals 3, yellowish, marked with purple, the lip nearly white. Stamens and pistil united into a column. May-June.

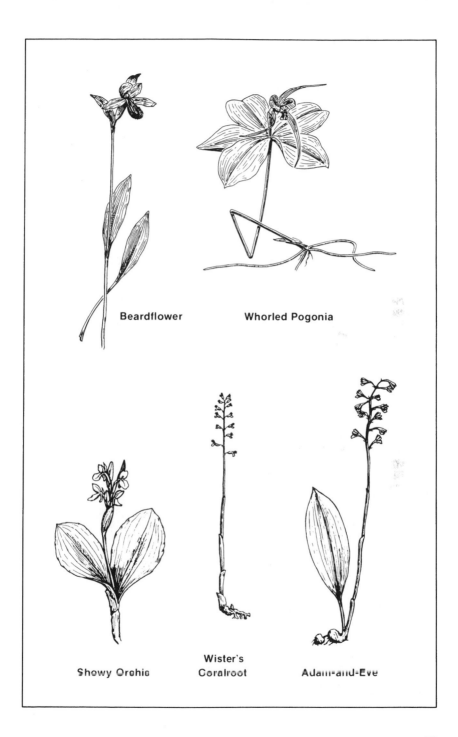

Beardflower   Whorled Pogonia

Showy Orchis   Wister's
                 Coralroot   Adam-and-Eve

Pink Lady's Slipper. Moccasin Flower
Cypripedium acaule Ait.

The Pink or Stemless Lady's Slipper is easily recognized by its pink flower, borne at the summit of a stalk (scape) from the base of which grow 2 large opposite leaves. The lip is in the form of an inflated pouch, similar in appearance to an old-fashioned moccasin. This plant is perhaps the most highly prized wild orchid in West Virginia because of its beautiful color and odd appearance and it has been almost exterminated in the State through thoughtless picking. It grows in dry woods.— Scape 6 to 16 inches high. Leaves many-nerved and plaited. Flowers solitary, fragrant. Sepals apparently 2, greenish-brown. Petals greenish-brown, the lip crimson-pink, rarely white, inflated. May-June.

Showy Lady's Slipper
Cypripedium reginae Walt.

This, the most beautiful of our native orchids, is so rare in West Virginia, and so in danger of being completely exterminated by the ruthlessness of flower-pickers, that it is advisable to keep secret the exact localities in which it has been found. At present it is known only from Greenbrier and Tucker counties growing in wet woods or swamps.—Stems downy, 1 to 2½ feet high. Leaves large, ovate, pointed, plaited. Flowers large, fragrant. Sepals apparently 2, white. Petals 3, the two lateral white, the lip white, pink in front, an inch and a half long. Late May or June.

Small Yellow Lady's Slipper
Cypripedium parviflorum Salisb.

In bogs, shaded banks, and rich woods, particularly in the mountain counties, this beautiful orchid may occasionally be found, having, says Mrs. Dana, an alert, startled look due to its long, slender, wavy, perianth parts. In richness of color and fragrance it is superior to its larger relative.—Stem 1 to 2½ feet high, downy, leafy to the top. Leaves alternate, oval, many-nerved. Flowers 1 or 2. Sepals apparently 2, greenish, tinged with purple. Petals 3, the 2 lateral greenish, tinged with purple, the lip golden-yellow, ¾ to 1¼ inch long. May-June.

Large Yellow Lady's Slipper
Cypripedium pubescens Willd.

This species is rather generally distributed in moist woods over the State, but is nowhere common. As in all other members of this genus, careless picking has caused it to become rare. Even transplanting to gardens is not recommended, except under special conditions, because of the lack of success that often attends such well-meant undertakings.—Stem about 2 feet high, more downy and more robust than the preceding. Leaves alternate, oval, plaited. Flowers large, showy, 1 or 2 on each plant. Sepals 3 but joined so as to appear as two, greenish or brownish, tinged with purple. Petals 3, the 2 lateral colored like the sepals, the lip golden brown, 1½ to 2 inches long. May-July.

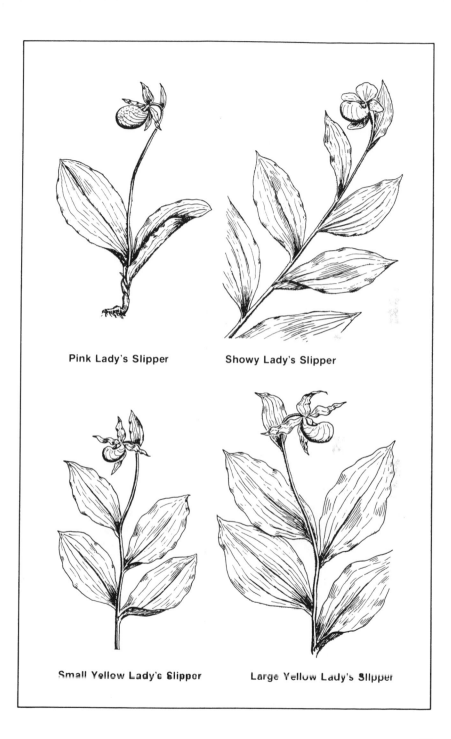

Pink Lady's Slipper

Showy Lady's Slipper

Small Yellow Lady's Slipper

Large Yellow Lady's Slipper

Spring Beauty
Claytonia virginica L.

The scientific name for this plant honors John Clayton who lived near Richmond in the early part of the 18th century and is sometimes referred to as the first American botanist. The Spring Beauty is one of our earliest plants and its exquisite coloring makes it especially charming. It is quite common in most parts of the State.—Stem more or less reclining, arising from a deep tuber. Leaves 2, opposite, long and narrow. Flowers pretty, in a loose raceme. Sepals 2. Petals 5, white with pink veins, or rose color, with deep veins. Stamens 5. Pistil 1, with style 3-cleft at the summit. March-May.

Carolina Spring Beauty
Claytonia caroliniana Michx.

This species is quite similar to the preceding, but is somewhat larger and more erect with larger but fewer flowers. It can be most readily recognized however, by its broader leaves. It is not so common as the preceding, but is found in most parts of the State, in the same situations.—Leaves oblong or oval-lanceolate. Petals 5, rose-color with deeper veins. March-May.

Wild Ginger
Asarum canadense L.

The Wild Ginger forms large beds of dark green velvety leaves arising from long rootstocks whose ginger-like odor and taste suggested the common name for the plant. It is very common in West Virginia and may be found in rich moist woods in every county. The flowers are not showy and are often hidden close to the ground beneath dead leaves.—Leaves usually 2, heart-shaped, long-stalked. Flower solitary, on a short stalk from between the 2 leaves. Calyx 3-parted, dull purplish-brown. Corolla none. Stamens 12. Pistil 1, with 6 stigmas. April-May.

Great Chickweed
Stellaria pubera Michx.

Half a dozen or more kinds of Chickweed are found in West Virginia, but most of them are common weeds which came to us from the Old World. This, the largest and prettiest of them, however, is a native of the Alleghenies, common in every county in our State, growing in moist rocky woods.—Stem weak, more or less reclining on the ground. Leaves ovate. Flowers white, ½ inch broad. Sepals 5. Petals 5, but deeply 2-parted, appearing 10. Stamens 10. Pistil 1. April-May.

Common Chickweed
Stellaria media (L.) Cyrill.

This is one of the commonest weeds in West Virginia, an introduction from Europe, growing in dooryards, gardens, and along roadsides in all parts of the State. Its principal flowering period is in early spring, but flowers may be found on warm days even in mid-winter and, when the weather is not too dry, in mid-summer as well.—Stem weak, lying almost flat upon the ground. Leaves very small. Flowers white, less than 1/3 inch broad. Sepals 5. Petals 5, so deeply parted as to look like 10. Stamens 3-7. Pistil 1, with 3 styles. January-December.

Stitchwort. Narrowleaf Chickweed
Stellaria graminea L.

The stitchwort is another introduction from Europe and has become common in grassy places in many parts of the State. Its weak stem, when supported by surrounding plants, may grow to a height of 1 to 2 feet. The name stitchwort refers to an ancient belief that a drink made from the plant would cure a "stitch" in the side. It can easily be separated from most of the chickweeds by its narrow leaves.—Stem ascending or reclining. Leaves narrow. Flowers white. Sepals 5. Petals 5, deeply 2-cleft. Stamens 10 or fewer. Pistil 1, with 3 stigmas.

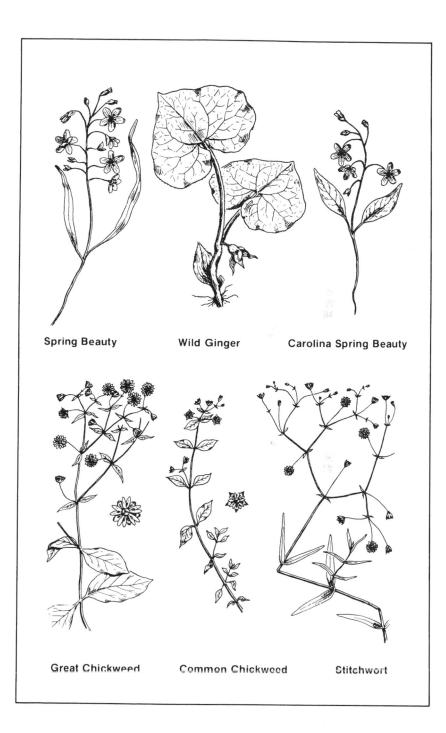

Spring Beauty   Wild Ginger   Carolina Spring Beauty

Great Chickweed   Common Chickweed   Stitchwort

Common Mouse-Ear Chickweed
Cerastium vulgatum L.

A common perennial weed in dooryards and fields, this is another introduction from Europe, sometimes becoming a troublesome pest. In general, *Cerastium* may be distinguished from *Stellaria* in producing 4 or 5 styles, whereas *Stellaria* has but 3. The stems are covered with sticky hairs.—Stems 6 to 18 inches high, spreading or reclining. Leaves hairy. Sepals 5. Petals 5, white, so deeply cleft as to appear like 10. Stamens 10 or fewer. Pistil 1, with mostly 5 styles. May-July.

Clammy Mouse-ear Chickweed
Cerastium viscosum L.

This is an annual plant, and while often found in moist grassy places, it is not so common as the last. It is generally smaller and even at maturity the flower-stalks are no longer than the sepals, whereas in the preceding species the mature flower-stalks are much longer than the sepals.—Stems less than 8 inches high, erect, hairy and clammy (sticky). Leaves ovate or oblong. Sepals 5, sharp-pointed. Petals 5, white, so deeply cleft as to appear like 10. Stamens 10 or fewer. Pistil 1, with usually 5 styles. May-June.

Nodding Chickweed. Powderhorn
Cerastium nutans Raf.

The Nodding Chickweed is another native species, not an introduction from the Old World as are many chickweeds. The ripe seedpods, inclining or nodding on the ends of the stalks, are shaped like a powderhorn, suggesting the common names. The plant occurs in rich moist soil of fields and roadsides throughout the State.—Stems annual, 6 to 24 inches tall. Flowers small, white. Sepals 5. Petals 5, deeply 2-parted. Stamens 10 or fewer. Pistil 1 with usually 5 styles. May-July.

Wild Pink
Silene pensylvanica Michx.

The Wild Pink finds its most suitable habitats on shaly or rocky soil in the valleys of the Potomac and its tributaries in eastern West Virginia, often hanging in vivid clusters from the edges of roadbanks. It is interesting to know that the pinks were so-called because of their "pinked" (notched) petals, rather than because of the color of their flowers.—Stems 4 to 8 inches high. Leaves opposite, those from the root wedge-shaped, those on the stem lance-shaped. Sepals united into a tube. Corolla of 5 pink petals, notched at the tip. April-June.

Fire Pink. Catchfly
Silene virginica L.

The Fire Pink is a showy plant, often found in shaly soil of dry, open woods in many parts of the State but particularly common in the hilly region from the Alleghenies westward. Its stems are covered with sticky hairs to which small insects become attached, suggesting the English name Catchfly.—Stems 10 to 20 inches high, slender, erect or reclining. Leaves lanceolate or oblong. Flowers few, loosely clustered, 1 to 2 inches broad. Calyx tube-shaped. Corolla of 5 deep crimson petals, each with 2 teeth at the end. Stamens 10. Pistil 1. May-June.

Sandwort
Arenaria serpyllifolia L.

The Sandwort is a common but inconspicuous little plant growing in sandy soil in many parts of the State.—Stems 2 to 6 inches high, in close clumps. Leaves ovate, small. Flowers small, in terminal leafy clusters. Sepals 5. Petals 5, white. Stamens 10. Pistil one, with usually 3 styles. May-August.

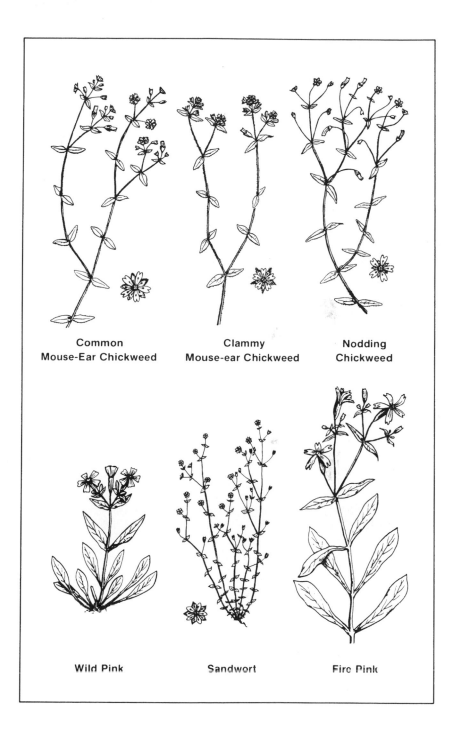

Common
Mouse-Ear Chickweed

Clammy
Mouse-ear Chickweed

Nodding
Chickweed

Wild Pink

Sandwort

Fire Pink

Yellow Pondlily. Spatterdock
Nymphaea advena Ait.

In slow streams and stagnant ponds throughout West Virginia, doubtless in every county, may be seen the very distinctive leaves and flowers of the Yellow Pondlily or Yellow Waterlily. The flowers lack the beauty and fragrance of many of the other waterlilies.—Leaves round or oblong, with a deep cleft at the base. Flowers 1 to 3 inches wide, cup-shaped, partly closed. Calyx of about 6 sepals, yellow, tinged with green or brown. Corolla of numerous petals, much shorter and hidden by the sepals. Stamens very numerous. Pistil 1, with a large circular stigma. April-September.

Marsh Marigold
Caltha palustris L.

The brilliant yellow flowers of the Marsh Marigold, appearing like large buttercups, are very common at high elevations in our mountain counties, in marshes, bogs and low ground along streams. They grow in great abundance, forming beds that spread over considerable areas. They are sometimes used as greens when coming into flower.—Stem hollow, glabrous, 1 to 2 feet high. Leaves rounded, heart-shaped or kidney-shaped. Flowers in terminal clusters. Sepals 5 to 9, golden yellow, resembling petals. Petals none. Stamens numerous. Pistils 5 to 10. April-June.

Golden Seal. Yellowroot
Hydrastis canadensis L.

The Golden Seal is a plant to be classed along with ginseng as being in danger of extermination due to the activities of herb collectors who dig the rootstocks for their medicinal value. Some mountain folk have been able to add appreciably to their annual cash income through sale of these dried "herbs." Formerly somewhat abundant in rich woods, especially in the mountain counties. The flower is not showy.—Stem about one foot high, arising from a knotty yellow rootstock. Leaves of two types, a single one from the rootstock and a pair of stem leaves near the flower. Flower solitary, greenish-white. Sepals 3, reddish-white, resembling petals but falling very early. Petals none. Stamens numerous. Pistils several. April-May.

Goldthread
Coptis trifolia (L.) Salisb.

The bright yellow thread-like rootstocks of this little plant give it its common name. It is found only in high elevations in the mountains, growing in moss of sphagnum bogs or about the roots of spruce trees in cool moist woods. The flowers are not large and the delicate beauty of the plant is partly due to its shiny dark green leaves.—Scape slender, 3 to 5 inches high. Leaves evergreen, divided into 3 leaflets. Flower solitary, white. Calyx of 5 to 7 petal-like sepals which quickly fall. Corolla of 5 to 7 small petals. Stamens 15 to 25. Pistils 3 to 7. May-July.

Dwarf Larkspur
Delphinium tricorne Michx.

Thr bright violet-blue clusters of the Dwarf Larkspur are noticeable features of rich woods in every county of the State west of the Appalachians. Occasional white-flowered plants are found. The common name is in reference to the interesting shape of the showy flowers.—Stems 6 to 36 inches high, arising from a cluster of tuberous roots. Leaves deeply parted, with narrow lobes. Flowers in terminal racemes. Calyx of 5 blue sepals, the upper one prolonged backward into a long spur. Corolla of 4 irregular blue petals, the upper two extended backward in spurs enclosed by the spur of the calyx. Stamens numerous. Pistils 3. April-May.

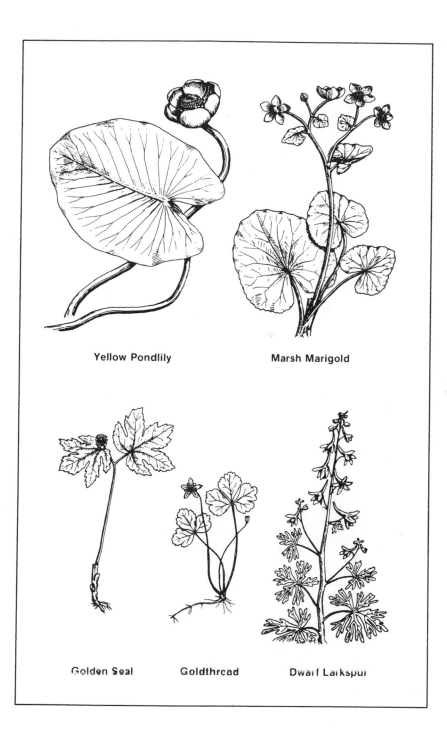

Yellow Pondlily

Marsh Marigold

Golden Seal   Goldthread   Dwarf Larkspur

Wood Anemone. Windflower
Anemone quinquefolia L.

These delicately beautiful little flowers are common in rich spring woods, especially in our mountain counties, often growing in extensive colonies. The name Windflower refers to its appearance in the windy season. The tremulous beauty of the slender anemones has been celebrated by poets from the days of ancient Greece down to our own Whittier and Bryant.—Stem 5 to 10 inches high. Leaves 3 in a whorl, each 3-parted. Flower solitary, nearly an inch broad. Sepals 4 to 7, petal-like, white, often tinged with pink outside. Petals none. Stamens numerous. Pistils 15 to 20. April-May.

Columbine
Aquilegia canadensis L.

The lovely, daring Columbine secures a foothold against the most precipitous rocky cliffs and is one of our most widely known and highly regarded spring flowers, common in every county of the State. The name Aquilegia is from the Latin word for eagle, in allusion to the spurred flowers, while the word columbine refers to a dove, perhaps referring to a fancied resemblance of the flower to the head of that bird.— Stem 1 to 2 feet high, branched. Leaves much-divided, the leaflets lobed. Flowers large and showy, nodding on the ends of the branches. Sepals 5, regular, petal-like, red. Petals 5, with spreading red lips, prolonged backward into hollow spurs red without and yellow within. Stamens numerous. Pistils 5. April-June.

Rue Anemone
Anemonella thalictroides (L.) Spach.

The Rue Anemone is common throughout the State in dry open woods. Like the Wood Anemone it is often called Windflower, its slender-stalked flowers easily shaken by the winds of early spring. It can be transplanted and is quite adaptable to cultivation in wild flower gardens.—Stem 4 to 12 inches high. Leaves divided into rounded leaflets. Flowers conspicuous, clustered in a terminal umbel. Sepals 5 to 10, white or sometimes pinkish, petal-like. Petals none. Stamens numerous. Pistils 4 to 15. March-June.

False Rue Anemone
Isopyrum biternatum (Raf.) T. & G.

The False Rue Anemone is found only along the Ohio River from Parkersburg south, but is often quite abundant there, in moist woods and thickets.—Stem 4 to 12 inches high. Leaves ternately divided. Flowers about ½ inch broad. Sepals 3 or 6, white. Petals none. Stamens 10-40. Pistils 2-20. April-May.

White Baneberry
Actaea alba (L.) Mill.

The White Baneberry is widely distributed in rich woods throughout the state, most common on the western slopes of the mountains.—Stem 1 to 2 feet high. Leaves compound, the leaflets sharply toothed. Flowers numerous, small, in ellipsoid terminal racemes. Sepals 4 or 5, small, falling off as the flower opens. Petals 4 to 10, small, white, spatulate. Stamens numerous, with white filaments. Pistil 1, Berry white. April-June.

28

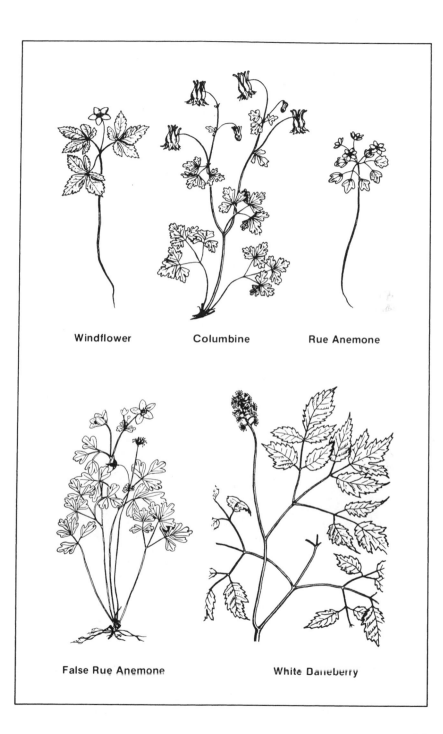

Windflower   Columbine   Rue Anemone

False Rue Anemone   White Daneberry

Sharplobed Hepatica
Hepatica acutiloba DC.
The hairy flower buds of the Hepatica push up through the brown leaves of the forest floor, oft'times in mid-March while snowdrifts yet linger nearby. If we rule out the curious Skunk Cabbage and the "everblooming" chickweeds, the delicately beautiful Hepatica may well be called the first flower of spring. The name Hepatica is from the Greek for liver, referring to the shape of the lobed leaf.—Scape short, hairy. Leaves with 3 pointed lobes, appearing later than the flowers and persisting through the winter until the next spring. Flower solitary. Calyx of 6 to 12 blue, white or pinkish petal-like sepals, easily mistaken for a corolla because of the 3 small green leaves just beneath, which resemble a calyx. Corolla none. Stamens numerous. Pistils several. March-May.

Roundlobed Hepatica
Hepatica americana (DC.) Ker.
Both species of Hepatica are common in woods throughout the State, often growing side by side. Except for the shape of the leaves the two species are almost identical. The ancients believed that plants having structural features resembling in any way organs of the human body possessed remedial properties useful in curing diseases of those organs; hence the Hepatica or Liverleaf was said to be useful in treatment of diseases of the liver.—Leaves with 3 rounded lobes, arising directly from the roots. Sepals 6 to 12, blue, white, or pinkish. March-May.

Early Meadowrue
Thalictrum dioicum L.
The delicate, drooping, fern-like foliage of this plant is noticeable in rocky woods or shady banks throughout the spring months, in virtually all parts of the State. The small greenish flowers are like drooping tassels.—Stem 1 to 2 feet high. Leaves divided into many lobed pale drooping leaflets. Flowers numerous, unisexual. Calyx of 4 or 5 small petal-like, purplish or greenish-white sepals. Corolla none. Stamens numerous, with yellowish anthers. Pistils 4 to 14, occurring on different plants from the stamens. April-May.

Leatherflower
Clematis viorna L.
In rich soil of thickets or forest margins the Leatherflower may occasionally be found in any part of the State but is so infrequent that its discovery is noteworthy. The curious, rather large, leathery flowers, nodding on long flower stalks, serve to identify the plant most readily. The stems are climbing and often woody towards the base.— Stems long, climbing by the bending of the petioles. Leaves opposite, pinnate, the leaflets 3 to 7. Sepals 4, purple, about an inch long, very thick. Petals none. Stamens numerous. Pistils numerous. May-August.

Dwarf Clematis
Clematis albicoma Wherry
The Dwarf Clematis is an endemic species, that is, one whose geographic range is restricted to a narrow area. It finds its suitable habitat on the shale barrens, lying in the inter-mountain valleys of the Alleghenies, in the eastern part of the State. The word *albicoma* means white hair, referring to the white hairy plumes on the ripe fruits.—Stem 1 to 2 feet high, erect (not climbing). Leaves ovate, entire or 3-lobed. Flowers solitary. Sepals 4 or 5, purplish. Stamens numerous. Pistils numerous. May-June.

Purple Virgin's Bower
Clematis verticillaris DC.
This resident of the northwoods reaches the southernmost limit of its range on high, cold, rocky mountain summits of West Virginia. It is a beautiful species and it is unfortunate that it is among our rarest plants.—Stem somewhat woody, climbing, 5 feet or more long. Leaves compound, with 3 ovate, pointed leaflets. Flowers produced singly on long stalks, very showy. Sepals 4, very thin, light purple, petal-like. Petals none. Stamens numerous. Pistils numerous.

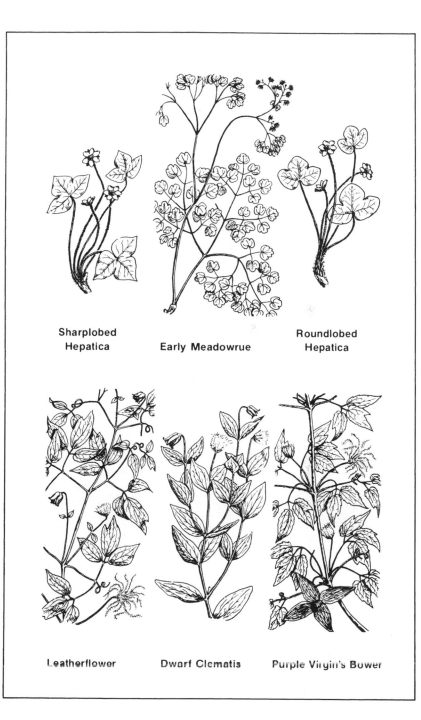

Sharplobed
Hepatica

Early Meadowrue

Roundlobed
Hepatica

Leatherflower

Dwarf Clematis

Purple Virgin's Bower

Kidneyleaf Crowfoot
Ranunculus abortivus L.

The word crowfoot is a name applied to members of the genus Ranunculus, in reference to the fact that many of them have leaves divided into three narrow segments, like the toes of a crow's foot. This is one of the earliest and commonest of all, being found in rich soil of shady hillsides and along streams, in every county of the State.—Stem 1 to 2 feet high. Leaves of two sorts, some of the lower kidney-shaped or heart-shaped, crenate, the upper divided into 3 narrow parts. Flowers numerous, small, ¼ inch broad, the receptacle hairy. Sepals 5. Petals 5, pale yellow. Stamens numerous. Pistils numerous. April-June.

Small-flowered Crowfoot
Ranunculus micranthus Nutt.

The Small-flowered Crowfoot is almost identical in appearance with the kidney-leaf crowfoot, but the stem is covered with long hairs and the receptacle is glabrous. It is less common but grows with the preceding species in open woods.—Stem 1 to 2 feet high, villous, arising from tuberous roots. Leaves of two sorts, some of the lower ones obvate, not deeply divided, the upper ones divided into 3 narrow leaflets. Flowers very small, ¼ inch broad. Sepals 5. Petals 5, light yellow. Stamens numerous. Pistils numerous. April-May.

Allegheny Crowfoot
Ranunculus allegheniensis Britton

The Allegheny Crowfoot resembles very closely in general appearance the two preceding species but has a glaucous stem and the achenes have a distinct curved beak, whereas the two above described have scarcely any beak at all. This species is more rare and is found principally in rich woods.—Stem 1 to 2 feet high, bearing very soft hairs. Lower leaves undivided, the upper 3-parted. Flowers very small, numerous. Sepals 5, yellow. Petals 5, pale yellow. Stamens numerous. Pistils numerous. April-May.

Hooked Crowfoot
Ranunculus recurvatus Poir.

The Hooked Crowfoot is also quite a common plant in West Virginia, growing in rich soil of open woods. The striking feature of the plant is the long recurved ("hooked") beak of the achene. The root leaves are large and rarely divided.—Stem ½ to 2 feet long, branching, hairy. Leaves on long petioles, broadly kidney-shaped, deeply 3-parted. Flowers small, numerous, 1/3 inch broad. Sepals 5, reflexed. Petals 5, pale yellow. Stamens numerous. Pistils numerous. April-June.

Green Hellebore
Helleborus viridis L.

This very early blooming plant is a native of Eurasia, cultivated in America as an ornamental, sometimes escaping and becoming established in the wild.—Stem 1 to 2 feet high. Leaves palmately. divided. Flowers solitary. Sepals 5, greenish-yellow, nearly an inch long. Petals 8 to 10, tiny. Stamens numerous. Pistils 3 to 10. February-April.

Lesser Celandine
Ranunculus ficaria L.

This lovely member of the buttercup family is a native of Europe, but has escaped and become abundant along Macfarlan Creek, in Ritchie County.—Stem 4 to 12 inches high. Leaves cordate-ovate. Sepals 3. Petals 8 to 12, yellow, lustrous. Stamens and pistils numerous. April-June.

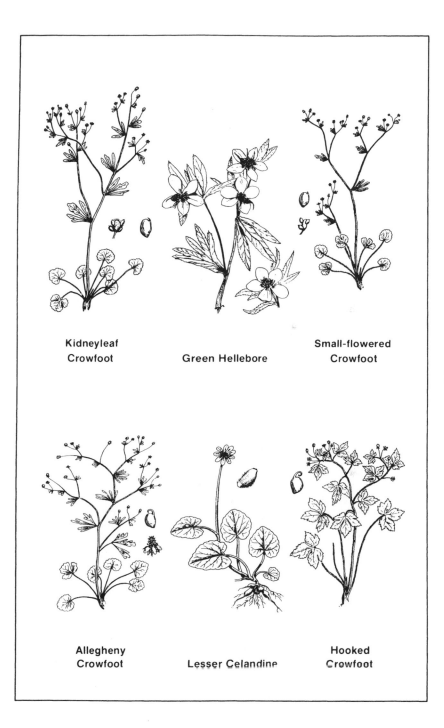

Kidneyleaf
Crowfoot

Green Hellebore

Small-flowered
Crowfoot

Allegheny
Crowfoot

Lesser Celandine

Hooked
Crowfoot

33

Creeping Buttercup
Ranunculus repens L.

The Creeping Buttercup is a small plant spreading along the ground by runners and often forming large colonies in rich moist soil. It is grown in flower gardens, usually in the double-flowered form and is perhaps not a native to West Virginia but merely an escape from cultivation.—Stems low, creeping. Leaves 3-divided, variously cleft, sometimes with white splotches. Flowers showy, nearly an inch broad. Sepals 5. Petals 5, deep yellow. Stamens numerous. Pistils numerous. May-July.

Tall Buttercup
Ranunculus acris L.

This is the buttercup common in meadows and roadsides throughout the State, but especially in mountainous regions, introduced from Europe. The name buttercup refers to the color and appearance of the flowers, and is frequently found in European and American literature. In general, the large-flowered species of *Ranunculus* are called buttercups, while the name crowfoot is applied to small-flowered species.— Stem 2 to 3 feet high, branching, hollow, somewhat hairy. Leaves 3-divided, the divisions again parted or cleft. Flowers showy, about an inch broad. Sepals 5. Petals 5, bright golden yellow, glossy, each with a nectar-bearing scale at the base. Stamens numerous. Pistils numerous. May-August.

Swamp Buttercup
Ranunculus septentrionalis Poir.

The Swamp Buttercup is found along shady banks, flood plains of streams, and in marshy ground, and is common throughout the State. The stems are ascending, or on wet ground forming long runners which take root at the ends. The habitat is generally sufficient to separate this species from the closely similar Hispid Buttercup, which is normally found on dry hillsides.—Stem 1 to 2½ feet high, upright or sometimes trailing on the ground and forming runners. Leaves 3-divided, the divisions variously cleft and at least the central one stalked. Flowers showy, one inch broad. Sepals 5. Petals 5, bright orange-yellow. Stamens numerous. Pistils numerous. May-July.

Bulbous Buttercup
Ranunculus bulbosus L.

Like the Tall Buttercup, this is an introduced species but it is not nearly as widespread in West Virginia as that species, and does not normally form large colonies. It is found occasionally in fields and roadsides in most parts of the State. The easiest way of distinguishing it is by the bulb-like base of the stem.—Stems about one foot high, arising from a bulb-like base. Leaves 3-divided or 3-cleft, the divisions wedge-shaped, cleft and toothed. Flowers showy, more than one inch broad. Sepals 5. Petals 5, 6, or 7, deep glossy yellow. Stamens numerous. Pistils numerous. May-July.

Hispid Buttercup
Ranunculus hispidus Michx.

The Hispid Buttercup is found in dry, open woods throughout West Virginia and is one of the most common of the early buttercups. The stems are densely hairy ("hispid") and arise from thickened, fibrous roots. This species resembles somewhat the Swamp Buttercup, but does not develop the long runners characteristic of that species.—Stem 6 to 16 inches high, spreading but not trailing on the ground. Leaves 3-divided, the divisions variously cleft. Flowers showy, about 1 inch broad. Sepals 5. Petals 5, bright yellow. Stamens numerous. Pistils numerous. March-May.

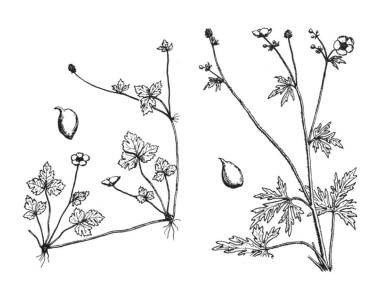

Creeping Buttercup   Tall Buttercup

Swamp Buttercup   Bulbous Buttercup   Hispid Buttoroup

Blue Cohosh. Pappooseroot
Caulophyllum thalictroides (L.) Michx.

The Blue Cohosh is common in deep rich woods of early spring, in every county of the State. The stem is dark colored and smooth, blue-glaucous when young. The name Pappooseroot refers to its use by the American Indians.—Stem 1 to 1½ feet high, from knotty rootstocks. Leaves two, a large ternately compound one, and usually a smaller one just below the flowers. Flowers greenish yellow, clustered at the summit of the stem. Sepals 6. Petals 6, thick, gland-like, much smaller than the sepals. Stamens 6. Pistil 1. April-May.

Twinleaf
Jeffersonia diphylla (L.) Pers.

In the early days of April the lovely Twinleaf may be found blooming in deciduous woods of every county in West Virginia. The scientific name was given in honor of Thomas Jefferson, while the common name refers to the two equal leaflets, one of the most distinctive features of the plant.—Scape 6 or 8 inches high, one-flowered. Leaves arising from the root, long-stalked. Flower showy, an inch broad. Sepals 4, falling off as the flower opens. Petals 8, white. Stamens 8. Pistil 1. April-May.

Mayapple
Podophyllum peltatum L.

The Mayapple is one of our best known and most widely distributed plants, growing in rich soil of woods and fields in every part of the State. Almost every child has played with the curious umbrella-like leaves and sought the partly hidden pretty white flowers or the ovoid, edible but rather unpleasantly flavored yellow "apples" which ripen in July.—Stems 1 to 2 feet high, the flower-less stems terminated by one large round leaf, the flowering stems bearing two one-sided leaves. Flower 1, large, nodding from the fork between the two leaves. Sepals 6, quickly falling. Petals 6 to 9, white. Stamens 6-9. Pistil 1. April-May.

Celandine
Chelidonium majus L.

The Celandine is a plant introduced from Europe but frequently found naturalized in this country. It occurs in rich moist soil of roadsides and waste places, sometimes in woods like a native plant. The stem contains an orange-colored sap.—Stems 1 to 2 feet high, weak, branching. Leaves pinnately divided or parted. Flowers pretty, ¾ inch broad, clustered. Sepals 2. Petals 4, deep yellow. Stamens 16 to 24. Pistil 1. April-September.

Bloodroot
Sanguinaria canadensis L.

The Bloodroot is one of our loveliest early spring flowers. The snowy white flowers appear in rich woods after only a few warm sunny days. It is welcomed by all as an indication that spring has finally come, but the flower is best enjoyed by leaving it on the stalk, since a mere touch is all that is required to cause the petals to fall. The thick rootstock, as well as the scape and leaves, contains a crimson juice which gives the common name.—Flowers terminal, the buds at first swathed by the young leaves. Sepals 2, falling early. Petals 8 to 12. Stamens about 24. Pistil 1. March-May.

Celandine Poppy
Stylophorum diphyllum (Michx.) Nutt.

In damp woods of most parts of the State hillsides are occasionally brightened by this handsome flower, which in general appearance suggests the Celandine. However, the flowers are more than twice as large as those of that species, and this is a native plant, not an introduced one.—Stem low. Leaves of the stem two, opposite, deeply incised, those from the root incised or divided. Flowers showy, 2 inches broad. Sepals 2. Petals 4, deep yellow. Stamens many. Pistil 1. April-May.

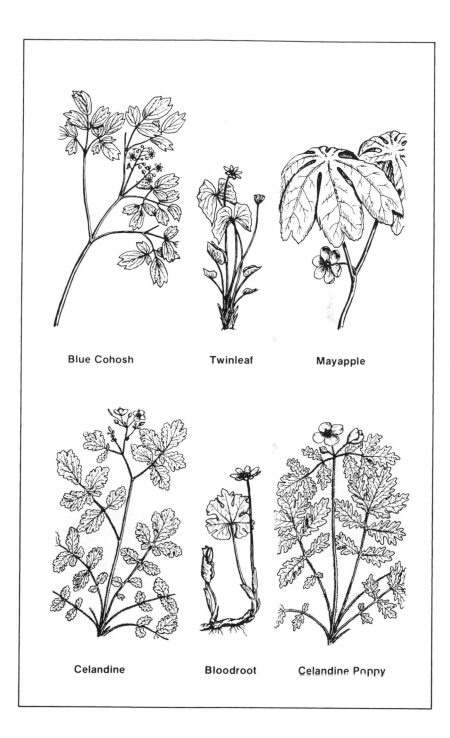

Blue Cohosh   Twinleaf   Mayapple

Celandine   Bloodroot   Celandine Poppy

Pale or Yellow Corydalis
Corydalis flavula (Raf.) DC.

The shy little Pale Corydalis is a common but inconspicuous plant found in rich moist woods in all parts of the State, flowering in early spring. The word Corydalis is the Greek name for a lark and refers to the little spur of the flowers.—Stem 6 to 15 inches high. Leaves light bluish-green, compound, the leaflet dissected. Flowers clustered, irregular, about a quarter inch long. Sepals 2, very small. Petals 4, pale yellow, the spur short. Stamens 6, somewhat united into 2 sets. Pistil 1. March-May.

Pink Corydalis
Corydalis sempervirens (L.) Pers.

The graceful foliage and delicately beautiful flowers of the Pink Corydalis are characteristic of rocky clefts in late spring and summer woods in many parts of West Virginia, but particularly in the mountain counties. They often occur also in recent clearings or in areas newly burned-over.—Stem 6 inches to 2 feet high, glaucous. Leaves glaucous, compound, dissected. Flowers numerous, in loose clusters. Sepals 2, small, scale-like. Petals 4, pink, tipped with yellow, with one short spur. Stamens 5. Pistil 1. May-August.

Squirrelcorn
Dicentra canadensis (Goldie) Walp.

This delicate little spring flower is a familiar inhabitant of rich woods in all parts of the State. The name refers to the numerous yellow grain-like tubers the size of peas from which the plant arises and which are said to be eaten by squirrels. It often forms large colonies in spring woods characterized by blue-green leaves and occasional flowering plants. The Latin name means two-spurs.—Scape slender, 5 to 9 inches high. Leaves blue-green, ternately compound and dissected. Flowers numerous in clusters, fragrant. Sepals 2, very small. Petals 4, greenish-white, tinged with pink. Stamens 6. Pistil 1. April-May.

Wild Bleedingheart
Dicentra eximia (Ker.) Torr.

This wild relative of the beautiful Bleeding Heart of flower gardens is common on dry, open, rocky or shaly mountain sides, principally on the eastern slopes of the Alleghenies. The plants are easily transferred to gardens and compete in beauty favorably with many of our introduced flowers.—Scape 6 to 18 inches high. Leaves compound, lobed. Flowers slender, heart-shaped, clustered in panicles. Sepals 2, very small. Petals 4, pink or red, rarely white. Stamens 6. Pistil 1. May-September.

Dutchman's Breeches
Dicentra cucullaria (L.) Bernh.

This is one of the favorites among our early-blooming plants, the odd-shaped flowers and rich green foliage contributing a real spring-like aspect to the landscape of rich woods in which they grow. The common name is easily explained by the shape of the flowers, which are familiar in every county of West Virginia. They are easily transplanted.—Scape 5 to 10 inches high, arising from a scaly bulbous base. Leaves ternately compound, finely cut. Flowers numerous, irregular, heart-shaped. Sepals 2, very small. Petals 4, white, tipped with yellow, 2-spurred. Stamens 6. Pistil 1. April-May.

38

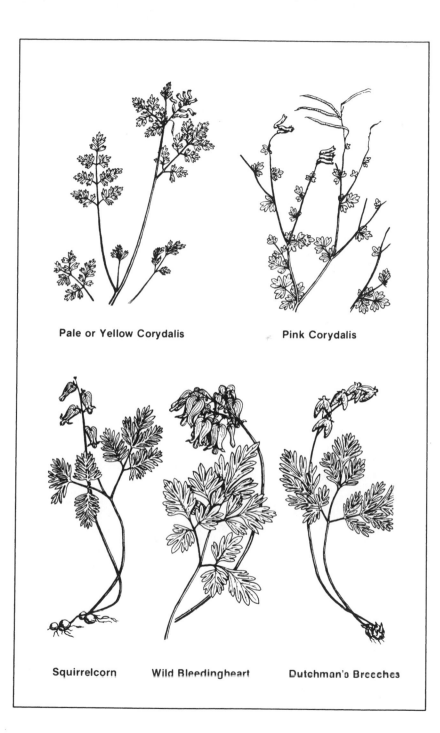

Pale or Yellow Corydalis   Pink Corydalis

Squirrelcorn   Wild Bleedingheart   Dutchman's Breeches

Field Cress
Lepidium campestre (L.) R. Br.

A common weed throughout West Virginia in fields, roadsides, and gardens, the field cress is a representative of the great and widely distributed mustard family. The mustards have a corolla with 4 petals spreading to form a cross and suggesting the word Cruciferae, the Latin name for the family. Most members of the family have a pungent, pleasant flavor. The field cress was introduced from Europe.—Stem erect, 10 to 18 inches high. Leaves clasping the stem by an arrow-shaped base, the root leaves in a rosette at the base of the stem. Flowers small, clustered at the summit of the plant. Sepals 4. Petals 4, white. Stamens 6, four long ones and two shorter. Pistil 1. May-July.

Peppergrass. Birdseed
Lepidium virginicum L.

A common weed of fields and roadsides, the Peppergrass, unlike the Field Cress, is a native of this country. Birds are very fond of these seeds and they are sometimes collected for feeding to canaries.—Stem 6 to 24 inches high. Leaves with a tapering base, not arrow-shaped, mostly incised. Flowers small, clustered at the summit of the stem. Sepals 4. Petals 4, white. Stamens 2. Pistil 1. May-November.

Whitlowgrass
Draba verna L.

This little plant, a native of Europe, is one of our very earliest spring flowers, growing in roadsides and waste places in all parts of West Virginia, although it does not attract much attention because the flowers are small. The name refers to an early belief that the plant was useful in curing whitlow, an inflammation of the fingers. The flowers are cleistogamous, that is, fertilized in the bud.—Scape one to three inches high. Leaves all from the root, in a rosette at the base of the stem. Flowers small, in racemes. Sepals 4. Petals 4, white. Stamens 6. Pistil 1. February-May.

Shepherd's Purse
Capsella bursa-pastoris (L.) Medic.

Both the Latin name and the English name of this plant allude to the triangular, deeply notched seed pods. It is a native of Europe which has become world-wide in its distribution and is found as a common weed in every county of West Virginia.—Stem low, branching. Leaves of two kinds, the root leaves clustered in a rosette, the stems leaves arrow-shaped at the base and clasping the stem. Flowers small, clustered. Sepals 4. Petals 4, white. Stamens 6, two shorter than the others, as is usual in the mustard family. Pistil 1. February-December.

Rocktwist
Draba ramosissima Desv.

Cliffs and rocky mountainsides, principally on the eastern slopes of the Alleghenies, are decorated in early spring with masses of white flowers of the Rocktwist, a native American relative of the Whitlowgrass. The name refers to the strongly twisted seed pods, which ripen during the summer.—Stems 4 to 16 inches high. Leaves toothed, dark green. Flowers showy, in corymbose clusters. Sepals 4. Petals 4, white. Stamens 6. Pistil 1. April-June.

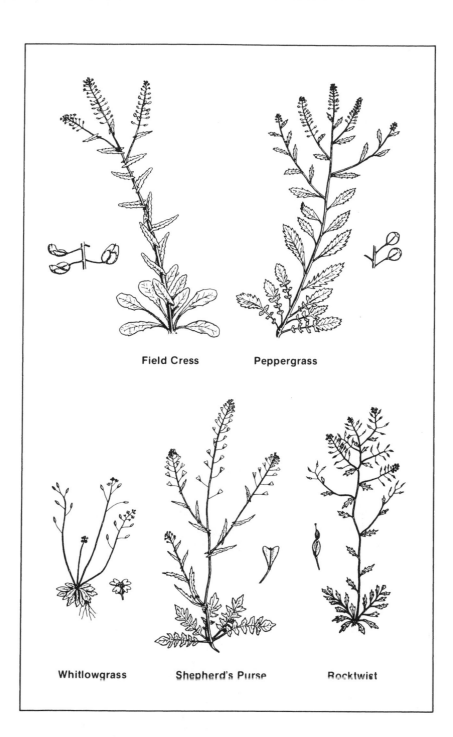

Field Cress   Peppergrass

Whitlowgrass   Shepherd's Purse   Rocktwist

41

Twoleaf Toothwort. Crinkleroot
Dentaria diphylla Michx.

The Crinkleroot, so named because of its wrinkled rootstocks, is common throughout West Virginia in rich woods and thickets. The rootstock is crisp and edible, with a pleasant pungent flavor.—Stem 8 to 15 inches high, bearing two leaves. Leaves divided into three toothed leaflets. Flowers in a terminal cluster. Sepals 4, soon falling. Petals 4, white. Stamens 6, two shorter than the others. Pistil 1. May.

Slender Toothwort
Dentaria heterophylla Nutt.

The Slender Toothwort is found in rich woods in many parts of West Virginia but is not nearly as common as the next species. The basal leaves are quite different in appearance from the stem leaves, whereas in the common toothwort the basal leaves, if present, are similar to the stem leaves.—Stem 10 to 14 inches high, arising from peppery rootstocks. Basal leaves 3, the leaflets ovate; stem leaves 2 or 3, the leaflets narrow, cut-toothed. Flowers showy, in a terminal raceme. Sepals 4, purplish-tinged. Petals 4, pinkish or lavender, half an inch long. Stamens 6. Pistil 1. April-May.

Cutleaf Toothwort
Dentaria laciniata Muhl.

The Toothwort is one of the commonest spring flowers of the State, but, strangely, many people do not know it by name. Like the Crinkleroot, it has an edible, peppery rootstock. The name Toothwort is the English rendering of the scientific name of the plant, and refers to the deeply toothed leaflets. It occurs in rich woods in every county of the State.—Stem 8 to 15 inches high, bearing 3 leaves. Leaves divided into 3 deeply cut-toothed leaflets. Flowers in a terminal cluster. Sepals 4. Petals 4, white or pinkish. Stamens 6. Pistil 1. April-May.

Sicklepod
Arabis canadensis L.

Sickle-shaped pods 2 or 3 inches long attract attention to this plant through the summer, its principal habitat being rocky open woodlands, where it is frequent in most parts of the State. The flowers are not conspicuous and the plant is seldom noticed in spring.—Stem upright, 2 to 4 feet high. Leaves sessile, hairy, the lower ones toothed. Flowers small, clustered, on hairy pedicels. Sepals 4. Petals 4, greenish-white. Stamens 6. Pistil 1. May-August.

Lyreleaf Rockcress
Arabis lyrata L.

The lyrate-pinnatifid basal leaves of this early Rockcress provide ready means of identification against the rocky banks where it is generally found.—Stem erect, 4 to 16 inches high. Root leaves pinnatifid, in a rosette at the base of the plant; stem leaves narrow, tapering. Flowers small, clustered. Sepals 4. Petals 4, pure white. Stamens 6. Pistil 1. March-May.

Smooth Rockcress
Arabis laevigata (Muhl.) Poir.

The Smooth Rockcress is frequently found in rocky places throughout the State. It differs from the sicklepod in having the pedicels smooth instead of hairy, and the stem leaves partly clasping by a heart-shaped base.—Stem upright, 1 to 2 feet high. Leaves lance-shaped or linear, clasping. Flowers small, clustered. Sepals 4. Petals 4, greenish-white. Stamens 6. Pistil 1. April-May.

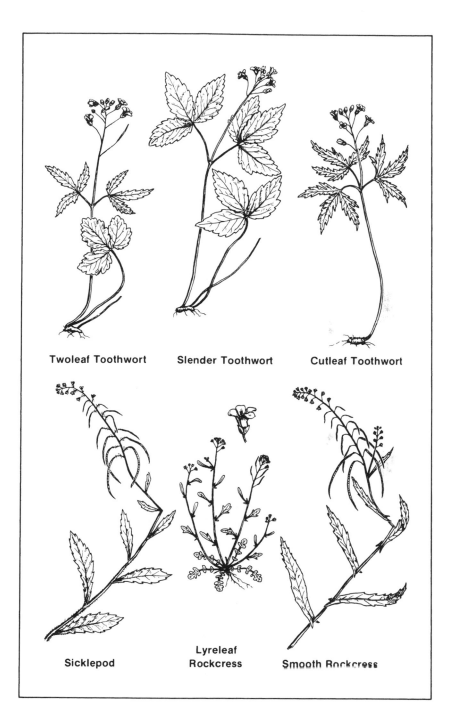

Twoleaf Toothwort   Slender Toothwort   Cutleaf Toothwort

Sicklepod   Lyreleaf Rockcress   Smooth Rockcress

Hairy Bittercress
Cardamine hirsuta L.

The Hairy Bittercress is found occasionally in most parts of the State, generally in moist places and waste ground. The leaves are mostly basal and the pods are an inch long or a little more. Otherwise this species is closely similar to the Small-flowered Bittercress.—Stem erect, 3 to 24 inches high. Leaves mostly radical, pinnately compound with 5 to 11 leaflets, hairy on the upper surfaces. Flowers small, clustered. Sepals 4. Petals 4, white. Stamens 4. Pistil 1. March-May.

Pennsylvania Bittercress
Cardamine pennsylvanica Muhl.

This Bittercress is a very common plant in moist ground throughout the State. It is very similar to the less common small-flowered bittercress, differing from that species in having oblong leaflets rather than linear. The pungent bitter taste of the foliage is sometimes communicated to milk when cows eat it in the spring.—Stem 8 to 36 inches high, essentially glabrous. Leaves pinnately compound, with 7 to 11 oblong leaflets. Flowers small, clustered. Sepals 4. Petals 4, white. Stamens usually 6, 4 long and 2 short ones. Pistil 1. April-June.

Small-flowered Bittercress
Cardamine parviflora L.

The Small-flowered Bittercress is occasionally found on dry rocky banks, roadsides and waste places throughout the State. This species differs from the closely related hairy bittercress in having a leafy stem, whereas the hairy bittercress has nearly all its leaves at the base of the plant. The pods are short, only about half an inch long.— Stem very slender, leafy, 2 to 15 inches high. Leaves compound, those of the stem with very narrow leaflets, the root leaves with oval leaflets. Sepals 4. Petals 4, white. Stamens usually 6. Pistil 1. April-May.

Purple Cress
Cardamine douglassii (Torr.) Britt.

The Purple Cress is common in shady wet places in most parts of the State, especially so in the mountains, and is easily distinguished from other members of the genus by its showy purple flowers. This plant is closely related to the Springcress. However, the present species blooms 2 to 3 weeks earlier.—Stem 4 to 10 inches high, arising from a tuberous base. Leaves simple, those from the root nearly orbicular, the others ovate or oblong. Flowers clustered, about a half inch broad. Sepals 4, purple-tinged. Petals 4, rose-purple. Stamens 6. Pistil 1. April-May.

Round-leaved Watercress
Cardamine rotundifolia Michx.

The weak branching stem of the Round-leaved Watercress is found along cool shady streams in the Alleghenies, where it often falls over, roots at the nodes or forms long runners. The leaves are simple or 3-foliolate, the blades being more or less rounded, with wavy margins and somewhat heart-shaped at the base. The plants have a pleasant pungent flavor.—Stem weak, decumbent, from fibrous roots. Sepals 4. Petals 4, white. Stamens 6. Pistil 1. May-June.

Springcress
Cardamine bulbosa (Schreb.) BSP.

The Springcress is so called because it normally appears around the borders of springs or in wet meadows. It is very similar to the Purple Cress, differing principally in the color of the flowers. It is found in most parts of West Virginia.—Stem upright, tuberous at the base, 6 to 20 inches high, arising from a slender, tuber-bearing rootstock. Leaves simple, those from the root oblong or ovate, those of the stem oblong or lanceolate. Flowers ½ inch broad, clustered. Sepals 4. Petals 4, white. Stamens 6. Pistil 1. May-June.

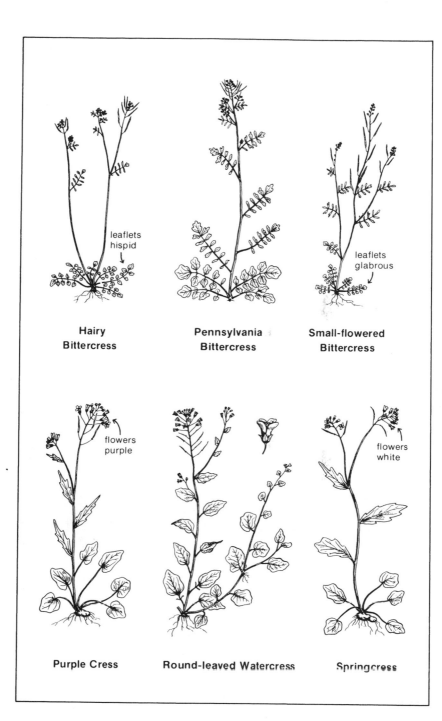

Hairy Bittercress

leaflets hispid

Pennsylvania Bittercress

Small-flowered Bittercress

leaflets glabrous

Purple Cress

flowers purple

Round-leaved Watercress

Springcress

flowers white

Watercress
Nasturtium officinale R. Br.

Watercress is not a native of North America but, introduced from Europe for its edible leaves, it has made itself at home in many cool, swiftly flowing brooks, and is scarcely to be regarded as a stranger. Its fresh pungent leaves are much used for greens or condiments. In West Virginia it is found chiefly in the counties to the east of the Alleghenies.—Stem spreading on the water or mud and rooting. Leaves divided into 3 to 11 roundish leaflets. Flowers rather small, clustered. Sepals 4. Petals 4, white. Stamens 6. Pistil 1. April-November.

Field Mustard
Brassica campestris L.

Several species of yellow-flowered mustards are found growing as weeds in cultivated fields in the late spring and summer throughout West Virginia, most of them introductions from Eurasia.—Stem 1 to 3 feet high, glabrous and glaucous; biennial. Leaves lanceolate or oblong, lobed or pinnatifid, the upper ones entire or dentate, sessile and clasping the stem by an auricled base. Flowers less than half an inch broad. Sepals 4. Petals 4, yellow. Stamens 6. Pistil 1. April-October.

Hedge Mustard
Sisymbrium officinale (L.) Scop.

The Hedge Mustard is a common weed in waste places, introduced, like many other members of the mustard family, from Europe. It is quite an unsightly weed and further obnoxious because it is a host for the clubroot fungus of cabbage.—Stems erect, 1 to 3 feet tall. Leaves sharply incised, with lobes turned backwards. Flowers small, clustered. Sepals 4. Petals 4, yellow. Stamens 6. Pistil 1. April-July.

False Flax
Camelina microcarpa Andrz.

This is an introduction from Europe, where it is often found in flax and other cultivated fields. It was formerly believed that flax degenerated into this species, as wheat was believed to change into cheat. It is found in West Virginia most commonly in the mountain counties.—Stem slender, 1 to 2½ feet high. Leaves lanceolate, sessile, auricled. Flowers small, in racemes. Sepals 4. Petals 4, yellow. Stamens 6. Pistil 1. May-July.

Purplerocket
Iodanthus pinnatifidus (Michx.) Steud.

The pretty Purplerocket is a modest and little-known native member of the mustard family, being found in West Virginia only on shaded banks of streams in the Ohio Valley. The scientific name is a Greek word meaning a "violet-colored flower."—Stem glabrous, 1 to 3 feet high. Leaves roundish or ovate-lanceolate, the stem leaves auricled and with winged petioles. Flowers showy, clustered. Sepals 4. Petals 4, purplish. Stamens 6. Pistil 1. May.

Wintercress. Yellowrocket
Barbarea vulgaris R. Br.

Wheat fields and rich low grounds throughout the State are often covered in April and May with the bright yellow flowers of the Wintercress, one of the first of the field mustards to appear. It is exceedingly common and a serious weed in some places, although, since it is a biennial, it dies shortly after flowering. It is an important honey plant and is much visited by bees. The leaves are collected for late winter greens.— Stem smooth, 1 to 2 feet high. Leaves cut-toothed or the lower pinnately compound with 1 to 4 pairs of leaflets. Flowers rather large, showy, in racemes. Sepals 4. Petals 4, yellow. Stamens 6. Pistil 1. April-July.

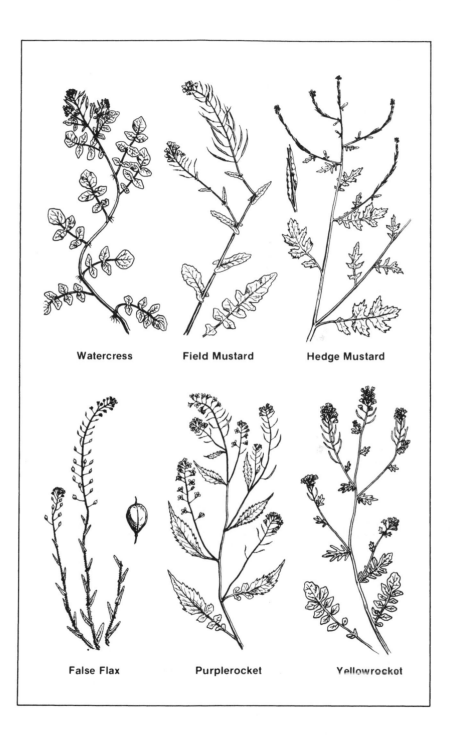

Watercress   Field Mustard   Hedge Mustard

False Flax   Purplerocket   Yellowrocket

Dame's Rocket
Hesperis matronalis L.

The distinctive fragrance of the flowers of this plant at dusk suggested the name Hesperis, the Greek word for evening or evening star. An old common name was Mother-of-the-Evening. It is a native of Europe, cultivated in American gardens, now widely escaped and established in thickets and woods along roadsides.—Stems up to a yard tall. Leaves lanceolate. Flowers numerous, showy. Sepals 4. Petals 4, purple. Stamens 6. Pistil 1. May-August.

Stonecrop
Sedum ternatum Michx.

The Common Stonecrop grows in moist, rocky woods in all parts of West Virginia. Its mossy tufts often appear on large boulders or against wet cliffs, like Tennyson's "flower in the crannied wall." The scientific name is from the Latin *sedere*, meaning to sit, alluding to the way in which the plants seem to sit upon rocks.—Stem spreading, in clumps, 3 to 6 inches high. Leaves flat. Flowers showy. Sepals 4 or 5. Petals 4 or 5, white. Stamens 8 or 10. Pistils 4 or 5. April-May.

Glaucous Stonecrop
Sedum glaucophyllum Clausen

On rocky mountains in the eastern part of the State the Glaucous Stonecrop may occasionally be found, but it is quite rare enough to be noteworthy. It can easily be separated from the Common Stonecrop by its alternate leaves and denser clusters of somewhat smaller flowers.—Stem 3 to 5 inches high, smooth. Leaves alternate, wedge-shaped, flat, glaucous. Flowers in a dense, 3-parted cluster. Sepals 4 or 5. Petals 4 or 5, white. Stamens 8 or 10. Pistils 4 or 5. May-June.

Lettuce Saxifrage
Saxifraga micranthidifolia (Haw.) Britton

The Lettuce Saxifrage is frequently found in bogs and swamps or along cool shady streams in the counties along the Alleghenies. It is much more common than the similar but less showy Swamp Saxifrage. It may be readily separated from that species by its coarsely toothed leaves.—Scape slender, 1 to 3 feet high. Leaves basal, sharply and coarsely toothed. Flowers in a loose panicle. Sepals 5. Petals 5, white. Stamens 10. Pistil of 2 separate or somewhat united carpels. May-June.

Early Saxifrage
Saxifraga virginiensis Michx.

In April dry hillsides and crevices in rocky cliffs become white with the blossoms of the Early Saxifrage. It is abundant in all parts of West Virginia. The word saxifrage is from the Latin *Saxum*, a rock, and *frangere*, to break, alluding to the way the plants grow in the clefts of the rocks and seem to break them.—Scape 4 to 12 inches high. Leaves clustered at the base of the stem. Flowers small, in an open cluster. Calyx 5-parted. Corolla of 5 white petals. Stamens 10. Pistil 1, with 2 styles. April-June.

Swamp Saxifrage
Saxifraga pensylvanica L.

The rare Swamp Saxifrage is occasionally found in the Allegheny Mountains, along cool mountain brooks and on wet rocks. Our only known stations in West Virginia are in Preston, Pocahontas and Tucker counties. It differs from the Lettuce Saxifrage in having greenish flowers and obscurely toothed leaves.—Scape 1 to 2 feet high. Leaves 4 to 8 inches long, narrowed at base into a broad petiole. Flowers small, in a terminal cluster. Calyx 5-parted. Corolla of 5 greenish petals. Stamens 10. Pistil 1, with 2 styles. April-June.

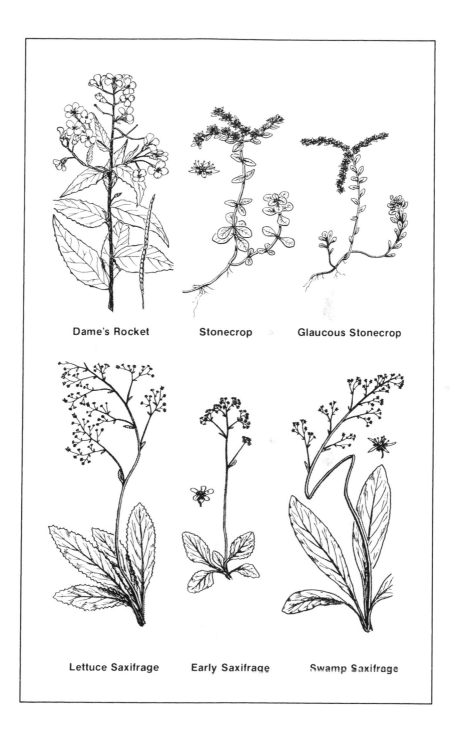

Dame's Rocket   Stonecrop   Glaucous Stonecrop

Lettuce Saxifrage   Early Saxifrage   Swamp Saxifrage

Bishop's Cap
Mitella diphylla L.

The delicately pretty flowers of the Bishop's Cap are familiar features in rich spring woods throughout the State. The scientific name means a little mitre, or cap, and this, as well as the common name, refers to the shape of the young seed pod. Miterwort is another name sometimes used, referring to the same feature. The small flowers consist of 5 fringed petals and resemble little stars.—Stem 6 to 12 inches high. Leaves heart-shaped, those on the stem two, opposite. Flowers many, in a slender raceme. Calyx 5-cleft. Corolla of 5 slender, deeply incised, white petals. Stamens 10. Pistil 1, with 2 styles. May.

Alumroot
Heuchera americana L.

There are several species of Alumroot in West Virginia but this is the commonest and one of the earliest. It is abundant in dry rocky woods in every county. The rootstock is quite astringent and produces an effect somewhat like alum when applied to the tongue.—Stem 2 to 3 feet high, somewhat hairy. Leaves heart-shaped, wavy-toothed, most of them arising from the base. Flowers numerous, in a long narrow cluster. Calyx bell-shaped, 5-cleft. Corolla of 5 small greenish or purplish petals. Stamens 5. Pistil 1, with 2 styles. May-August.

Foamflower
Tiarella cordifolia L.

The graceful white racemes of the Foamflower attract our attention in rich rocky woods throughout the entire State, giving an appearance somewhat like foam on a mountain stream. This plant is a close relative of the Bishop's Cap and is sometimes called False Miterwort, in reference to the shape of the pistil.—Stem 4 to 16 inches high, bearing only one or two small leaves. Leaves mostly arising from the rootstock. Flowers in a raceme, petals white. Stamens 10, long and slender. Pistil 1, with 2 styles. April-June.

Indian Physic
Gillenia trifoliata (L.) Moench.

This pretty plant, the root of which was used by the Indians as a physic, is common in fields, meadows and open woods throughout the State. It has no value to the modern physician since he has many remedies much superior to it. The name Bowman's-root, sometimes used for this plant, refers to an early medical practitioner, William Beaumont, who made regular use of it.—Stem 2 to 4 feet high, smooth, branching, reddish. Leaves 3-foliate, the leaflets ovate-lanceolate. Flowers terminal, in loose panicles. Calyx 5-toothed, reddish. Corolla of 5 pale rose color or white petals. Stamens 10 to 20. Pistils 5, slightly cohering with each other at the base. May-July.

Goatsbeard
Aruncus dioicus (Walt.) Fern.

This odd plant is familiar to residents of all parts of the State, since it is common in rich soil of banks and ravines. The flowers are produced in a long straggling, more or less drooping panicle, thought by the ancients to resemble a goat's beard.—Stem 3 to 7 feet tall, smooth, slender. Leaves pinnately compound, the leaflets large, ovate. Flowers small, in an open panicle. Calyx of 5 sepals united at the base. Corolla of 5 small narrow white petals. Stamens numerous. Pistils 3 or 4. May-July.

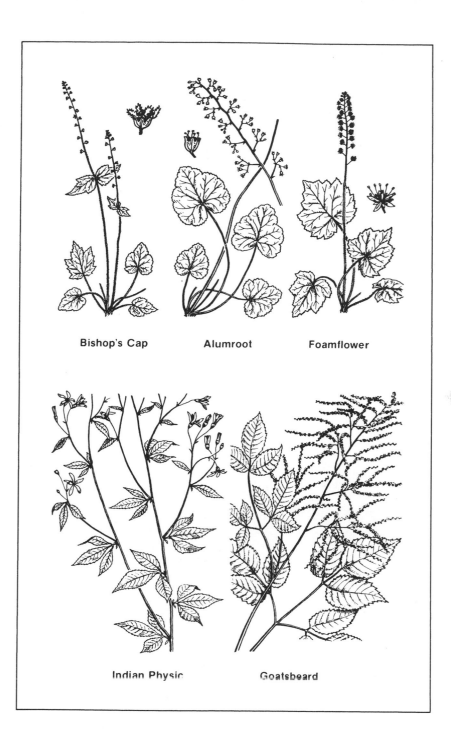

Bishop's Cap   Alumroot   Foamflower

Indian Physic   Goatsbeard

Wild Strawberry
Fragaria virginiana Duchesne

The Wild Strawberry is so well known in all parts of West Virginia that it needs no description. It grows in fields, meadows and waste places throughout the State. The flower is fragrant, whence the scientific name, but the delicious red fruit is especially sought and has a flavor surpassing that of the cultivated plants.—Stems prostrate on the ground, rooting at the nodes, the flowers and leaves arising from the roots. Leaves compound, with 3 coarsely serrate leaflets. Flowers showy, clustered in cymes. Calyx 5-cleft. Corolla of 5 white petals. Stamens many. Pistils many. April-June.

Cinquefoil
Potentilla canadensis L.

Dry fields and roadsides throughout West Virginia are dotted during spring with the bright flowers of Cinquefoil, which looks somewhat like a yellow-flowered wild strawberry. The common name is derived from the French *cinque feuilles*, five leaves.—Stem slender, prostrate on the ground, or suberect. Leaves divided into 3 leaflets but apparently 5 by the parting of the lateral leaflets. Flowers ½ inch broad, growing singly from the axils of the leaves. Calyx 5-cleft, with bracts between each tooth, thus appearing 10-cleft. Corolla of 5 yellow petals. Stamens many. Pistils many. May-July.

Barren Strawberry
Waldsteinia fragarioides (Michx.) Trattinick

This is another plant with the general appearance of a strawberry, but like the cinquefoil, it produces only a dry fruit, whence the common name. It is fairly abundant in shady fields in the mountain counties.—Scape low. Leaves compound, of 3 wedge-shaped leaflets. Flowers ½ inch or more broad, in clusters. Calyx 5-cleft. Corolla of 5 yellow petals. Stamens many. pistils many. May-June.

Spring Avens
Geum vernum (Raf.) T. & G.

This little plant, somewhat resembling a crowfoot, is common in thickets and shady hillsides throughout the State. The ripe achenes have long tails formed from the persistent, elongated styles.—Stem ascending, 6 to 24 inches high. Leaves lobed, in a rosette at the base of the stem and a few small ones on the stem. Flowers in loose clusters. Calyx 5-cleft. Corolla of 5 yellow petals. Stamens many. Pistils many. April-June.

Purple Avens
Geum rivale L.

This species is by no means common in West Virginia but occurs at several localities in high mountain swamps and wet glades. It is easily distinguished from other species of this genus by the color of its flower.—Stem erect, pubescent, 1 to 3 feet high. Leaves variable, the basal ones lyrate-pinnatifid, the stem leaves 3-foliolate or 3-lobed. Flowers few in a terminal cluster, nodding. Calyx 5-cleft. Corolla of 5 purple petals. Stamens many. Pistils many. May-July.

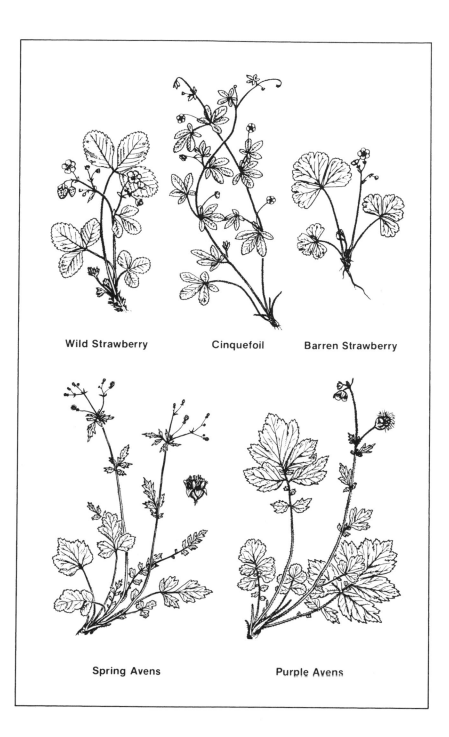

Wild Strawberry   Cinquefoil   Barren Strawberry

Spring Avens   Purple Avens

American Vetch
Vicia americana Muhl.

Both the common and scientific names of this plant go back to the old Latin name, Vicia. The American Vetch is a climbing plant found principally in West Virginia in the mountain counties. It is too scattered to have much value for grazing.—Stem climbing by a tendril at the end of the leaves. Leaves pinnately compound, with 10 to 14 ovate leaflets. Flowers irregular, in clusters. Calyx 5-cleft. Corolla purplish, more than a half inch long. Stamens 10, united by their filaments. Pistil 1. May-June.

Carolina Vetch
Vicia caroliniana Walt.

The Carolina Vetch is a trailing or climbing vine that is quite common throughout West Virginia, growing in open woods or along riverbanks. Like most flowers of the legume family, it has a papilionaceous corolla, that is, composed of two wing petals, a standard, and two petals joined to form a keel.—Stem trailing, nearly smooth. Leaves pinnately compound, with 8 to 24 leaflets. Flowers small, irregular, clustered. Calyx 5-cleft. Corolla of 5 pale blue petals. Stamens 10, somewhat united by their filaments. Pistil 1. April-June.

Milk Vetch
Astragalus distortus T. & G.

The bright rose-purple flowers of this rare little plant supply a surprising bit of color against the drab slopes of the shale barrens. This is a rare species, more common in the mid-west, and has been found in West Virginia only on shale barrens of the Eastern Panhandle.—Stems low, spreading, arising several together from one root. Leaves pinnately compound, with 17 to 25 leaflets. Flowers irregular, in a short spike. Calyx 5-toothed. Corolla of 5 bright purple petals. Stamens 10, somewhat united by their filaments. Pistil 1. April-May.

Mountain Clover
Trifolium virginicum Small

This rare clover, first discovered by John K. Small in 1892 on the slopes of Kate's Mountain, Greenbrier County, has been found in only 15 counties of West Virginia, Virginia, Maryland and Pennsylvania, always on dry shale barrens. It is one of the best known of the shale barren endemics.—Stem diffusely branched, the branches prostrate, villous. Leaves compound, the leaflets quite long and narrow. Flowers irregular, in large heads. Calyx 5-cleft. Corolla of 5 nearly white petals. Stamens 10, united by their filaments. Pistil 1. April-May.

Wild Lupine
Lupinus perennis L.

The long bright clusters of the Wild Lupine are found in shaly or sandy soil of open woods or fields, principally in the mountain counties. Both the pea-like flowers and the palmately compound leaves are quite attractive.—Stem erect, 1 to 2 feet high. Leaves compound, with 7 to 11 oblanceolate leaflets. Flowers irregular, showy, in terminal racemes. Calyx 5-cleft. Corolla of 5 bright blue petals. Stamens 10, united by their filaments. Pistil 1. May-June.

Veiny Pea
Lathyrus venosus Muhl.

This stout climbing plant is found in West Virginia along river shores and banks commonly in the southern counties. The English and the specific names refer to the strong venation of the leaflets.—Stem climbing, finely pubescent or nearly glabrous. Leaves pinnately compound, with 8 to 12 ovate leaflets. Flowers irregular, several in a cluster, more than half an inch long. Calyx 5-toothed. Corolla of 5 purple petals. Stamens 10, diadelphous. Pistil 1. May-July.

54

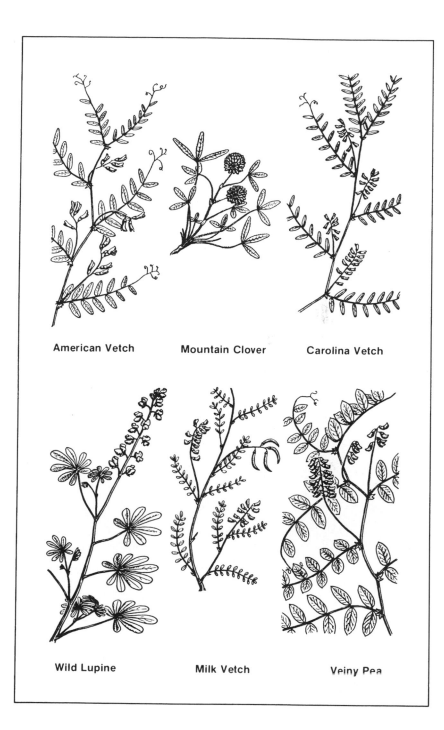

American Vetch   Mountain Clover   Carolina Vetch

Wild Lupine   Milk Vetch   Veiny Pea

Yellow Clover. Hop Clover
Trifolium agrarium L.

This little plant, an immigrant from Europe, is found in waste places and along roadsides in every part of West Virginia. The clovers are all characterized by a three-foliate leaf, and the name "clover" probably originated in the Latin *clava*, clubs, in reference to the fancied resemblance to the 3-pronged club of Hercules.—Stem 6 to 12 inches high, ascending. Leaves divided into 3 oblong leaflets, all 3 attached at the same point. Flowers small, irregular, in close heads. Calyx 5-cleft. Corolla of 5 yellow petals. Stamens 10, united. Pistil 1. May-September.

Low Hop Clover
Trifolium campestre Schreber.

The hop clovers are the only two of our West Virginia clovers with yellow flowers. This species can be separated from the preceding by its shorter stems and by the fact that the terminal leaflet is on a short stalk. The Low Hop Clover is common along roadsides and in sandy fields throughout the State.—Stem 4 to 6 inches high, spreading. Leaves divided into 3 wedge-oblong leaflets, the lateral ones at a short distance from the terminal one. Flowers small, irregular, in close heads. Calyx 5-cleft. Corolla of 5 yellow petals. Stamens 10. Pistil 1. May-September.

Rabbitfoot Clover
Trifolium arvense L.

This clover, like the two preceding, is an introduction from Europe and is especially noticeable on account of the oblong silky-pubescent heads, which suggest the name rabbitfoot. It is common in dry sandy, gravelly or shaly soil, particularly on the shale barrens in the eastern part of the State.—Stem silky, 4 to 16 inches high, erect, branching. Leaflets oblanceolate. Flowers small, irregular, in gray, soft-silky, ovoid-cylindrical heads. Calyx 5-cleft. Corolla of 5 yellow petals. Stamens 10, united by their filaments. Pistil 1. May-September.

Alsike Clover
Trifolium hybridum L.

This clover is named from Alsike, Sweden, and is another introduction from Europe. It is much sown for pasture and hay and has escaped to roadsides and waste places in all parts of West Virginia. It somewhat resembles the White Clover but the flower heads are pink around the edges and cream-colored in the center. It is not really a hybrid, although the Latin name seems to suggest it.—Stem 1 to 2 feet high, erect or ascending, not rooting at the nodes. Leaflets ovate. Flowers small, irregular, in close heads. Calyx 5-cleft. Corolla of 5 white or rose-tinted petals. Stamens 10, united. Pistil 1. May-October.

White Clover
Trifolium repens L.

This is one of our commonest clovers and is generally regarded as being native at least in the northern part of the United States, although it has been widely sown as a forage crop and on lawns, sometimes under the name Dutch clover. Like the other clovers, the flowers contain quantities of nectar and are visited by many kinds of bees. It is found everywhere in West Virginia in fields and roadsides.—Stem slender, spreading, the branches rooting at the nodes. Leaflets ovate. Flowers irregular, small, clustered in close heads. Calyx 5-cleft. Corolla of 5 white petals. Stamens 10, united by their filaments. Pistil 1. May-October.

Red Clover
Trifolium pratense L.

This clover, another immigrant from Europe, is one of our commonest and most useful species, being cultivated throughout the State as a forage plant and has widely escaped in fields and meadows.—Stem 6-24 inches high, hairy. Leaves of 3 oval leaflets, each marked on the upper side with a pale spot. Flowers small, irregular, in close heads. Calyx 5-cleft. Corolla of 5 red petals. Stamens 10. Pistil 1. May-September.

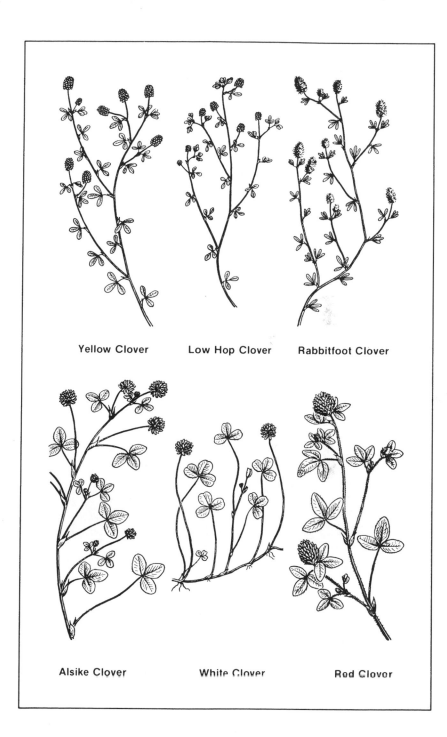

Yellow Clover   Low Hop Clover   Rabbitfoot Clover

Alsike Clover   White Clover   Red Clover

Herb Robert
Geranium robertianum L.

From spring until autumn, rocky woods and shady hillsides on the eastern slopes of the Alleghenies are decorated by the bright blossoms of the Herb Robert. The stems are reddish and covered with sticky hairs. A resinous secretion gives off a strong, somewhat unpleasant odor. The name is said to refer to Robert, Duke of Normandy, in whose time it was used, the story says, to cure a disease called "Robert's plague."—Stem 10 to 18 inches high, erect, branching. Sepals 5. Petals 5, red-purple. Stamens 10. Pistil 1, with 5 styles. May-October.

Wild Geranium
Geranium maculatum L.

The Wild Geranium is one of our most common woodland plants, being found in every county in the State. Because of the beak-like appearance of the fruit it is sometimes called cranesbill. The name maculatum ("spotted"), refers to the blotched appearance of the old leaves.—Stem erect, hairy, 1 to 2 feet high. Flowers an inch across. Sepals 5. Petals 5, light pink-purple. Stamens 10. Pistil 1, with 5 styles. April-July.

Carolina Cranesbill
Geranium carolinianum L.

The Carolina Cranesbill is somewhat similar in general appearance to the Herb Robert, although much paler in color. It occurs throughout the State, mostly in rocky or barren soil.—Stems 8 to 15 inches high, diffusely branched. Flowers small. Sepals 5. Petals 5, whitish or very pale pink. Stamens 10. Pistil 1, with 5 styles. May-June.

Upright Spotted Spurge
Euphorbia maculata L.

The members of the genus *Euphorbia* in West Virginia are herbs with a milky, acid juice. The flowers are very small and clustered within a cup-shaped involucre bearing appendages which are usually taken for the petals of the flower. This species is common in dry open soil throughout the State.—Leaves oblong, usually with red margins or a red spot. Flowers clustered within the cup-shaped involucre, formerly considered the flower itself; involucre 4-lobed, with white or red glands. Staminate flowers numerous, each consisting of a single stamen. Pistillate flower solitary in each involucre, consisting of a 3-lobed ovary. May-October.

Flowering Spurge
Euphorbia corollata L.

The Flowering Spurge has a cup-shaped, 5-lobed, involucre bearing showy white appendages which appear like petals. It is a handsome plant found in rich or sandy soil of open fields in every county of the State—Stem 1 to 3 feet high, erect. Leaves numerous, linear, lanceolate or ovate. Flowers clustered within the involucre. Staminate flowers numerous. Pistillate flower one in each involucre. May-October.

Variable Spurge
Euphorbia commutata Engelm.

Along streams and shady slopes the delicate Variable Spurge is a common but obscure member of our spring flora. The involucres are not showy as in some species of spurge and the pale green of the foliage blends with the leafy background.—Stem 6 to 12 inches high, branched. Leaves obovate, entire, the upper ones, about the flower clusters, roundish. Flowers clustered within the 4-lobed involucre, which bears crescent-shaped or 2-horned glands. Staminate flowers numerous, each consisting of a single stamen; pistillate flower one. March-July.

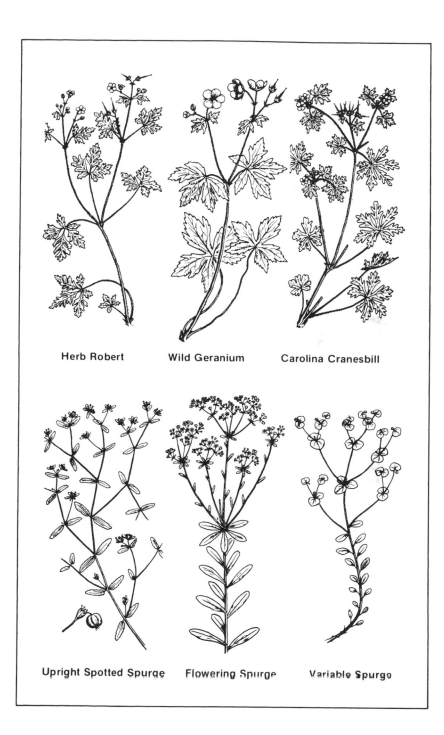

Herb Robert   Wild Geranium   Carolina Cranesbill

Upright Spotted Spurge   Flowering Spurge   Variable Spurge

59

Large Yellow Woodsorrel
Oxalis grandis Small

This is by far the largest species of Woodsorrel found in our region and is easily recognized by its large leaflets beautifully marked with brown-purple margins. It grows in sandy woods and alluvial soil, nowhere very abundant but found in all parts of the State.—Stem 12 to 18 inches high, generally softly pubescent. Leaves compound, with 3 large leaflets somewhat resembling clover. Flowers in cymes. Sepals 5. Petals 5, yellow. Stamens 10. Pistil 1. May-August.

White Woodsorrel
Oxalis montana Raf.

The White Woodsorrel is found in deep mountain woods where the forest floor is damp and mossy. There is probably no commoner nor more beautiful spring flower beneath the spruce trees in the higher Alleghenies. The same species grows in Europe and is said to have been the original Shamrock which St. Patrick of Ireland used to teach the concept of the Trinity in Unity.—Scape 2 to 5 inches high. Sepals 5. Petals 5, white, veined with rose-purple. Stamens 10. Pistil 1. May-July.

Lady's Sorrel
Oxalis corniculata L.

This yellow-flowered plant is a very common weed in all parts of West Virginia, along roadsides, in cultivated soil, and in grassy places. The name sorrel is from the Greek word meaning sour, in reference to the sour juice in the leaves and stem. The leaflets fold up against each other at night, in a "sleep movement."—Stem 1 to 6 inches high, erect or decumbent, perennial by runners. Flowers in cymes. Sepals 5. Petals 5, yellow. Stamens 10. Pistil 1, with 5 styles. April-November.

Violet Woodsorrel
Oxalis violacea L.

The Violet Woodsorrel seldom is very abundant but is found in practically every part of the State, at lower elevations than the white woodsorrel. In some respects it is still more beautiful than that species. It grows principally in rocky places or open woods, arising from a bulbous base.—Scape 5 to 9 inches high. Leaves divided into 3 leaflets. Sepals 5. Petals 5, violet. Stamens 10. Pistil 1, with 5 styles. May-June.

Seneca Snakeroot
Polygala senega L.

This little plant is fairly common in rocky soil, especially in mountain woods. It arises from a thickened knotty rootstock which is still extensively used in preparation of cough syrups. The common name recalls a once-powerful Indian tribe of central New York.—Stem 6 to 12 inches high. Leaves lanceolate, numerous. Flowers small, irregular, in a close spike. Sepals 5, 3 of them small and greenish, the others (called *wings*) much larger and colored like the petals. Petals 3, white. Stamens 6 or 8. Pistil 1. May-July.

Fringed Milkwort. Gaywings
Polygala paucifolia Willd.

John Burroughs said, concerning a company of these plants, that "it was as if a flock of small rose-purple butterflies had alighted there on the ground before us." They are quite common in woods or recent clearings throughout the mountain counties. The leaves somewhat resemble those of the wintergreen, suggesting the name Flowering Wintergreen, sometimes used.—Stem 3 or 4 inches high, arising from long prostrate or underground shoots. Flowers showy, 1 to 3 on each plant, over ½ inch long. Sepals 5, 3 of them small and greenish, the other 2 (the wings) larger, conspicuously fringed. Stamens 6. Pistil 1. May-June.

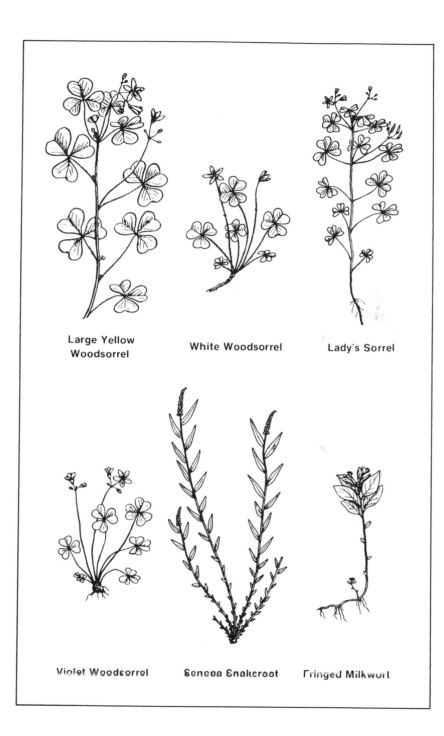

Large Yellow
Woodsorrel

White Woodsorrel

Lady's Sorrel

Violet Woodsorrel

Seneca Snakeroot

Fringed Milkwort

Downy Blue Violet
Viola sororia Willd.

The Downy Blue Violet is common in rocky woods throughout the State. It differs from the Common Blue Violet in being decidedly pubescent, although to a variable degree, whereas that species is typically quite glabrous, at least in the mature condition.—Scape often villous-pubescent. Leaves heart-shaped, crenate-serrate, the petioles villous. Flower solitary. Sepals 5. Petals 5, violet to lavender. Stamens 5. Pistil 1. April-July.

Common Blue Violet
Viola papilionacea Pursh.

This is the commonest of all our violets, growing in low ground, in woods, meadows, and waste places, in every county in the State. It is extremely variable in size, color of flowers, and shape of leaves. Children often call them Johnny-jump-ups and engage the spurred flowers in battles to see whose head falls first.—Scape usually glabrous. Leaves heart-shaped, the petioles glabrous or sparingly pubescent. Flower solitary. Sepals 5. Petals 5, deep violet, white or yellowish at the base. Stamens 5. Pistil 1. April-June.

Marsh Blue Violet
Viola cucullata Ait.

This species is the usual blue violet in open or somewhat shaded marshy places throughout the State. Its flowers closely resemble those of the preceding species, but are produced on long peduncles high above the leaves, whereas the peduncles of the Common Blue Violet are about the length of the petioles.—Scape glabrous. Leaves heart-shaped, crenate-serrate, glabrous. Flower solitary. Sepals 5. Petals 5, violet-blue. Stamens 5. Pistil 1. April-June.

Arrowleaf Violet
Viola sagittata Ait.

The Arrowleaf Violet may be recognized by its long-petioled arrow-shaped leaves. It occurs in moist or shady places or sometimes in dry fields, widely scattered throughout the State, but apparently local. The typical plant is glabrous, but pubescent forms are found and the species apparently intergrades with the Ovate-Leaved Violet.—Scape usually glabrous. leaves glabrous or finely pubescent, lanceolate or oblong lanceolate, toothed somewhat like an arrowhead at the base. Flower solitary. Sepals 5. Petals 5, violet-purple. Stamens 5. Pistil 1. April-May.

Birdfoot Violet
Viola pedata L.

The Birdfoot is our largest flowered and most beautiful wild violet. Its habitat is unusual as compared with most other violets, since it is found principally on dry slopes of the shale barrens in the eastern part of the State, where it startles the visitor with its unexpected beauty.—Scape nearly glabrous. Leaves 3-divided (somewhat resembling a bird's foot), the lateral division again 3-5-parted. Flower solitary, very showy. Sepals 5. Petals 5, the upper petals dark violet, the others lighter in color, or in some plants, all the petals of the same lilac-purple color. Stamens 5. Pistil 1. April-June.

Ovate-Leaved Violet
Viola fimbriatula Sm.

This species is rather common in dry, open places, particularly in the eastern part of the State. It can be recognized by its pubescent, ovate leaves which are sharply toothed near the base. Like most violets, it is quite variable in shape of the leaves and degree of pubescence.—Scape pubescent, exceeding the leaves. Leaves ovate, the basal lobes sometimes sharply toothed or incised. Flowers solitary. Sepals 5. Petals 5, violet-purple. Stamens 5. Pistil 1. April-May.

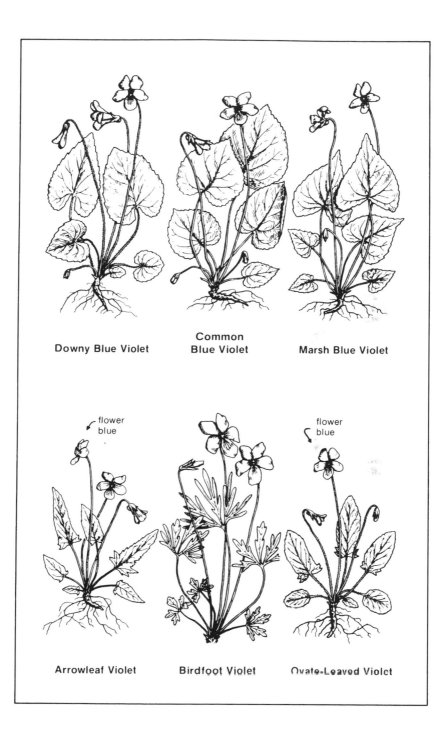

Downy Blue Violet

Common
Blue Violet

Marsh Blue Violet

flower
blue

flower
blue

Arrowleaf Violet

Birdfoot Violet

Ovate-Leaved Violet

63

Primrose-leaved Violet
Viola primulifolia L.

This species is found in marshy or sometimes in almost dry situations, mostly in the mountain counties. Brainerd says this is the largest species of the white violets of wet open places. It is most easily recognized by its ovate leaves.—Scapes usually glabrous, 2-10 inches high. Leaves oblong or ovate, crenate-serrate, usually glabrous. Flower solitary. Sepals 5, lanceolate. Petals 5, white with delicate purple veins. Stamens 5. Pistil 1. April-June.

Lanceleaf Violet
Viola lanceolata L.

This little white violet is found in bogs or moist meadows and differs from our other violets in having lanceolate leaves. We have records for only a few counties but its narrow leaves are easily overlooked and it is probable that it occurs in many other counties.—Scape 2 to 4 inches high. Leaves lanceolate, crenate, glabrous, about ½ inch wide by 1½ inches long at flowering time. Flower solitary. Sepals 5, lanceolate, acute. Petals 5, white. Stamens 5. Pistil 1. April-June.

Sweet White Violet
Viola blanda Willd.

This is the common white stemless violet of cool woods, and is found in all parts of the State. It is one of the smallest of our violets but Harned says it makes up for its small size by its sweet fragrance. It can easily be distinguished from its near-relative, the primrose-leaved violet, by the shape of the leaves.—Scape glabrous, exceeding the leaves. Leaves mostly 1 to 2 inches wide, deeply cordate, glabrous or nearly so, crenate. Flowers about ½ inch wide. Sepals 5. Petals 5, white, the 3 lower with delicate purple veins. Stamens 5. Pistil 1. April-May.

Early Yellow Violet
Viola rotundifolia Michx.

This is our only stemless yellow violet, but it is fairly common in cool, rich woods throughout the State, particularly in the mountain counties. It is also one of our earliest violets, often flowering during the latter part of March. It is easily recognized by the large round heart-shaped leaves which lie flat on the ground.—Scape 2 to 4 inches high. Leaves round-cordate, about 1 inch wide at flowering time, 4 to 5 inches wide in mid-summer. Flower solitary. Sepals 5. Petals 5, yellow. Stamens 5. Pistil 1. March-May.

Wild Pansy
Viola rafinesquii Greene

This is our only annual violet. It is often quite common locally in dry fields, banks, or open woods, in all parts of the State. Dr. Davis has observed that it frequently appears in thick, well-defined patches, as if sown, but that the following year the colonies may appear elsewhere in the same field, a characteristic that has been noted in other annuals.—Stems 4 to 6 inches high, nearly or quite glabrous. Leaves small, the earliest nearly orbicular, the later obovate; stipules large, leaf-like, lyrate-pinnatifid. Flowers small. Sepals 5, ovate, acute, ciliate. Petals 5, bluish-lavender to creamy white. Stamens 5. Pistil 1. March-May.

Long-spurred Violet
Viola rostrata Pursh.

This violet is common in rich woods in all parts of the State, but especially so in the mountains. It is easily recognized by the color of the flowers and the extremely long spur, nearly ½ inch long.—Stem glabrous or nearly so, 4 to 6 inches high. Leaves round, heart-shaped, serrate, more than 1 inch wide at flowering time. Flowers nearly 1 inch across or sometimes much smaller. Sepals 5. Petals 5, pale lilac, veined with blue, darker at the base. Stamens 5. Pistil 1. May-July.

64

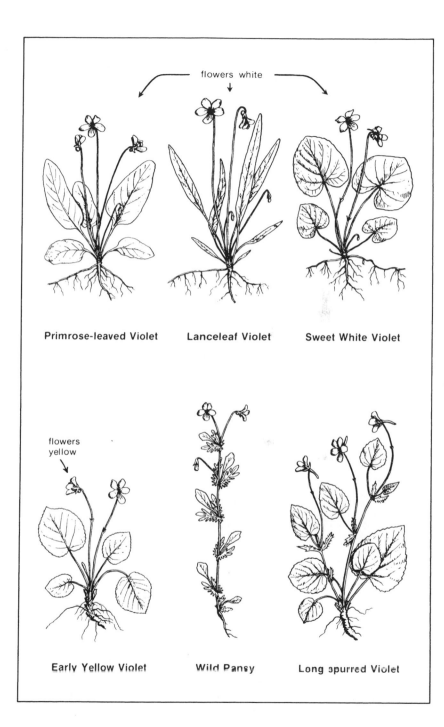

flowers white

Primrose-leaved Violet   Lanceleaf Violet   Sweet White Violet

flowers
yellow

Early Yellow Violet   Wild Pansy   Long spurred Violet

65

Downy Yellow Violet
Viola pubescens Ait.

This is our only leafy-stemmed yellow violet which is distinctly pubescent. It is frequently found in dry rich woods, particularly in the mountain counties.—Stem 8 to 15 inches high, downy. Leaves 2 to 4 near the summit, very broad, often 3 inches wide. Flowers small, on slender stalks. Sepals 5, lanceolate. Petals 5, golden yellow, with purple veins. Stamens 5. Pistil 1. April-May.

Halberdleaf Violet
Viola hastata Michx.

This violet can be easily recognized by its hastate leaves clustered near the top of the stem. It is rather frequent in dry woods, particularly in the mountain counties.—Stem 4 to 10 inches high, nearly glabrous. Leaves 2 to 4, near the summit, halberd-shaped, serrate. Flowers axillary. Sepals 5, linear-lanceolate. Petals 5, yellow. Stamens 5. Pistil 1. April-May.

Smooth Yellow Violet
Viola eriocarpa Schwein.

This is the common smooth leafy-stemmed yellow violet. It occurs in moist open woods in most parts of the State. It is quite similar in general appearance to the downy yellow violet, but is glabrous or nearly so.—Stems mostly in clusters of 2 or more, ascending, with a few or several spreading basal leaves. Leaves broadly ovate, crenate-dentate. Flowers axillary. Sepals 5, lanceolate. Petals 5, yellow. Stamens 5. Pistil 1. April-May.

Canada Violet
Viola canadensis L.

The Canada Violet occurs in rich woods throughout the State, especially in the mountain counties. It is easily recognized by its creamy-white flowers, purple-tinged on the back. It is doubtless our tallest and one of our loveliest violets.—Stem often 16 inches high. Leaves heart-shaped, serrate. Flowers appearing at intervals from spring throughout the summer. Sepals 5, long and narrow. Petals 5, white, with a yellow base, the spurred petal striped with fine dark lines, the backs of the upper petals flushed with purple. Stamens 5. Pistil 1. May-August.

Green Violet
Hybanthus concolor (Forster) Spreng.

The Green Violet, while a member of the violet family from the structure of its flowers, does not belong in the genus *Viola* and does not at all resemble the other violets in general appearance. It is found in rich woods, locally abundant in all parts of the State.—Stem 1 to 2½ feet high, more or less hairy. Leaves oblong, nearly entire, attenuate at apex. Flowers small and inconspicuous, in clusters of 1 to 3 from the axils of the alternate leaves. Sepals 5, linear. Petals 5, greenish-white, the lower one twice as broad as the others, swollen at the base, forming a rudimentary spur. Stamens 5. Pistil 1. April-June.

Striped Violet
Viola striata Ait.

This is our commonest leafy-stemmed violet, no doubt occurring in every county in the State in low moist situations, frequently along small streams. It is easily grown in flower gardens and spreads rapidly.—Stem 6 to 12 inches high when in flower. Leaves heart-shaped, finely crenate-serrate. Flowers ½ inch or more across. Sepals 5, ciliolate. Petals 5, creamy-white, veined with blue. Stamens 5. Pistil 1. April-May.

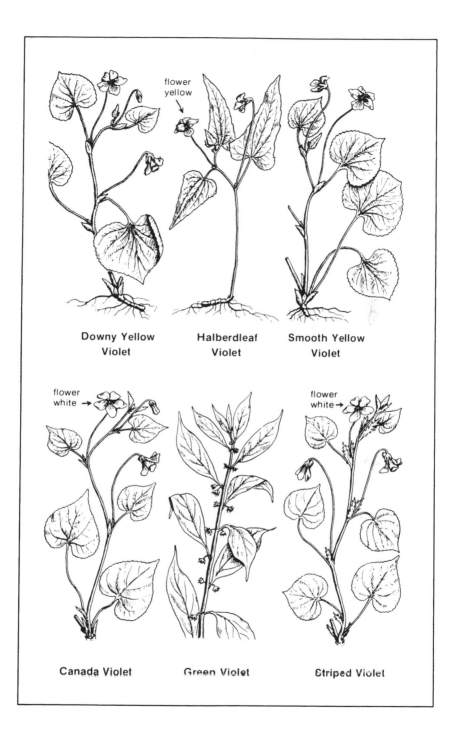

flower
yellow

**Downy Yellow
Violet**

**Halberdleaf
Violet**

**Smooth Yellow
Violet**

flower
white →

flower
white →

Canada Violet

Green Violet

Striped Violet

Hairy Sweet Cicely
Osmorhiza claytoni (Michx.) Clarke

This is a common woodland wild flower well known in all parts of the State. The roots are sweet-scented, but not so much so as the next species, which it closely resembles. The chief distinguishing character is the hairy stem.—Stem 1 to 3 feet high, hairy. Leaves ternate, hairy, the leaflets acuminate, toothed. Flowers small, in umbels. Calyx of 5 rudimentary teeth. Corolla of 5 small white petals. Stamens 5. Pistil 1, with 2 styles and an inferior ovary. May-June.

Smooth Sweet Cicely
Osmorhiza longistylis (Torr.) DC.

This species is also common in woods throughout the State and is well known to country children because of its sweet-scented, anise-like roots. Great care should be used not to confuse this plant with Water Hemlock, which it somewhat resembles and which is very poisonous.—Stem 1 to 3 feet high. Leaves twice or thrice compound. Flowers small, in a flat-topped umbel. Calyx of 5 rudimentary teeth. Corolla of 5 small white petals. Stamens 5. Pistil 1, with 2 styles and an inferior ovary. May-June.

Harbinger-of-spring
Erigenia bulbosa (Michx.) Nutt.

This is a very small plant with inconspicuous flowers quite easily overlooked but it deserves to be ranked along with our earliest spring flowers. It is found locally in moist woods throughout the State. The small dark anthers and tiny white petals suggest the name Pepper-and-salt, which is sometimes used for this plant.—Stem 3 to 9 inches high, arising from a deep round tuber. Leaves 1 or 2, ternately divided, the segments linear-oblong. Flowers small, few, in a leafy-bracted umbel. Calyx of 5 rudimentary teeth. Corolla of 5 white petals. Stamens 5. Pistil 1, with two styles and an inferior ovary. March-April.

Spreading Chervil
Chaerophyllum procumbens (L.) Crantz

Spreading Chervil, like Harbinger-of-spring, is a small, inconspicuous plant that is probably much more common than it seems because it often escapes attention. It is found in moist, usually shaded, ground, in most parts of the State. The fruit is long and slender, whereas that of the preceding species is nearly round. Otherwise they are closely similar.—Stem annual, slender, spreading, 6 to 20 inches long. Leaves ternately compound. Flowers small, in umbels. Calyx of 5 rudimentary teeth. Corolla of 5 white petals. Stamens 5. Pistil 1, with 2 styles and an inferior ovary. April-June.

Wild Sarsaparilla
Aralia nudicaulis L.

The compound leaves and rounded inconspicuous flower clusters of the Wild Sarsaparilla are frequently seen in moist woodlands in all parts of the State. It somewhat resembles ginseng, a closely related plant, and is sometimes called "fool's sang" by mountain folk. The long aromatic roots are used as a substitute for the true sarsaparilla.—Stem very short, barely rising above the ground, the single leaf and flower stalk arising separately. Leaf long-stalked, much-divided. Flowers small, in umbels. Calyx with very short teeth. Corolla of 5 greenish-white petals. Stamens 5. Pistil 1, with two styles and an inferior ovary. May-June.

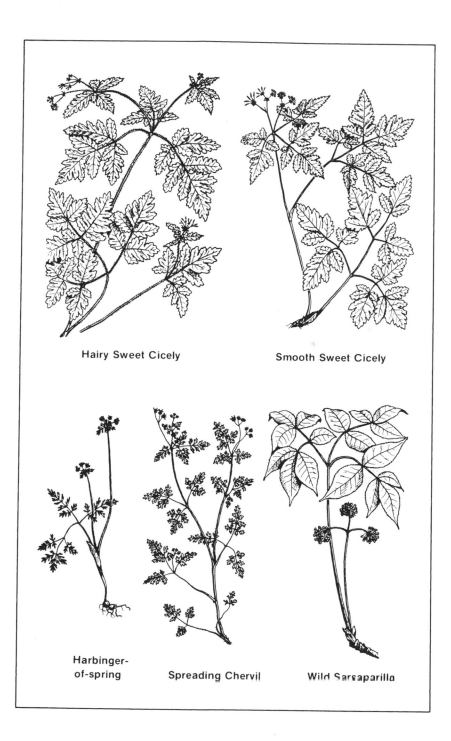

Hairy Sweet Cicely

Smooth Sweet Cicely

Harbinger-
of-spring

Spreading Chervil

Wild Sarsaparilla

Golden Alexanders
Zizia aurea (L.) Koch.

This is one of the earliest members of the parsnip family to appear in the spring. Its golden-yellow flower clusters are often seen along river-banks, in meadows and in rich woods, probably in every county of the State.—Stem 1 to 3 feet tall. Leaves ternately compound, those from the root with long petioles. Flowers small, in umbels. Calyx with 5 teeth. Corolla of 5 yellow petals. Stamens 5. Pistil 1, with 2 styles and an inferior ovary. April-June.

Mountain Pimpernel
Pseudotaenidia montana Mackenzie

The genus *Pseudotaenidia,* of which the Mountain Pimpernel is the only member, is most remarkable in that it occurs only on shaly slopes of the Alleghenies in West Virginia and neighboring states. It was first discovered by Mackenzie in 1903 on Kates Mountain at White Sulphur Springs, and is thus an entire genus first to be observed in this State.—Stem 1½ to 2½ feet high, glabrous. Leaves ternately compound, with entire leaflets. Flowers small, in umbels. Calyx with 5 short teeth. Corolla of 5 yellow petals. Stamens 5. Pistil 1, with 2 styles and an inferior ovary. May.

Trailing Arbutus
Epigaca repens L.

The waxy blossoms and delicious fragrance of the Trailing Arbutus are among the foremost joys of early spring. Appearing as they do when we are eagerly looking for the first signs of the re-awakening of plant life, they win unusually glad recognition. It is said that they were the first flowers to greet the Pilgrims after their fearful winter and were named by them Mayflowers. They prefer light sandy acid soil and are very difficult to move into flower gardens.—Stem prostrate or trailing, covered with rusty hairs. Leaves evergreen, rounded, heart-shaped. Flowers showy, white to dark pink. Calyx of 5 dry pointed sepals. Corolla united into a slender tube with 5 lobes. Stamens 10. Pistil 1, with a 5-lobed stigma. March-April.

Shooting Star
Dodecatheon meadia L.

The Shooting Star is an unusual but quite handsome plant common on mountain ridges and moist cliffs, particularly in the eastern and southern counties. The name refers to the manner in which the showy petals are abruptly recurved, a condition which has also suggested the name Indian Bonnet.—Scape 1 to 2 feet high. Leaves clustered at the base of the plant. Flowers showy, in an umbel. Calyx deeply 5-cleft. Corolla with a very short tube and 5 rose-color or white segments. Stamens 5. Pistil 1, with 1 style and stigma. April-June.

Starflower
Trientalis americana (Pers.) Pursh.

The Starflower is one of our most delicate and fragile little plants, arising from a horizontal, creeping rootstock. The whole effect of the leaf arrangement and snow-white blossoms is starry and pointed so that the common name is quite appropriate. The species is found throughout the State, but is common only locally.—Stem 3 to 9 inches high, smooth, erect. Leaves thin, pointed, in a whorl at the summit of the stem. Flowers one or more, delicate, star-shaped. Calyx generally 7-parted. Corolla white, generally 7-parted. Stamens 4 or 5. Pistil 1. May-June.

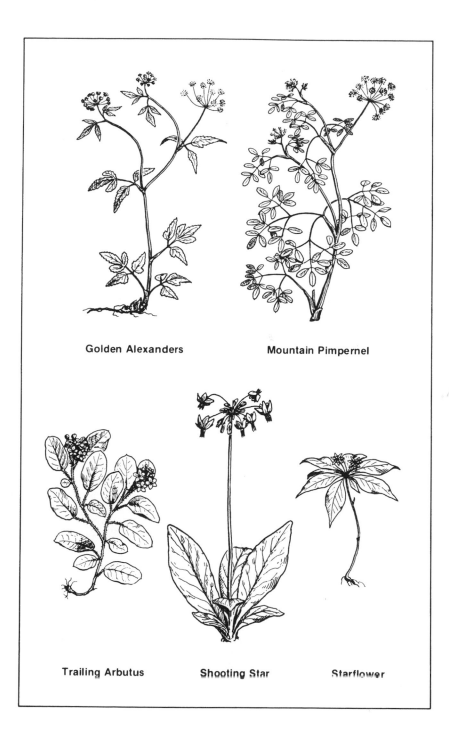

Golden Alexanders   Mountain Pimpernel

Trailing Arbutus   Shooting Star   Starflower

Periwinkle. Myrtle
Vinca minor L.

This plant is a native of Europe but widespread throughout West Virginia as an escape from gardens and around cemeteries. It is a small, slender, trailing plant with evergreen leaves. In this region it is often called Myrtle, although it is not the true myrtle, nor even in the myrtle family.—Stems prostrate on the ground, rooting and establishing new plants. Leaves firm, glossy. Flowers in the axils of the leaves. Calyx 5-parted. Corolla blue, 5-lobed. Stamens 5. Pistil with 2 distinct ovaries but united into a single style and stigma. March-June.

Buckbean
Menyanthes trifoliata L.

In late spring it is a rare privilege to find among the sedges and mosses of a mountain bog the beautiful white flowers of the Buckbean. The name was apparently given because of the habit of deer browsing the succulent leaves. It has been found in West Virginia only in Pocahontas, Preston, and Tucker counties.—Scape about 1 foot high. Leaves long-petioled, arising from the roots, divided into 3 leaflets. Flowers clustered along the scape. Calyx 5-parted. Corolla 5-cleft, white or reddish. Stamens 5. Pistil 1, with a 2-lobed stigma. April-June.

Pennywort
Obolaria virginica L.

One of the rarest finds of the early spring woods is the inconspicuous little Pennywort, its purplish-green blending so perfectly with the background as to make it very difficult to locate. It is found in widely separated parts of the State but only locally, and is nowhere abundant.—Stem 3 to 6 inches high, very smooth. Leaves opposite. Flowers solitary or in clusters of 3, less than ½ inch long. Calyx of 2 spreading sepals, resembling the leaves. Corolla 4-lobed, dull white or purplish. Stamens 4. Pistil 1, with a 2-lipped stigma. March-May.

Four-leaved Milkweed
Asclepias quadrifolia Jacq.

The Milkweeds are coarse plants with a milky juice, mostly blooming in summer fields. This is the earliest to flower in West Virginia, in open woods and thickets throughout the State.—Stem 1 to 3 feet tall. Leaves opposite, the uppermost in whorls of 4. Calyx 5-parted. Corolla pink or nearly white, 5-parted. Stamens 5, united. Pistils 2, developing into long follicles. May-July.

Shale Bindweed
Convolvulus purshianus Wherry

This unusual relative of the twining bindweeds grows upright and is usually not more than a foot high. Although it has a summer-blooming upright relative which is more common, this species is known only from the shale barrens of the eastern counties, hence should be listed among our rarer plants.—Stem erect, 8 to 12 inches high. Leaves auricled at the base, very velvety. Flowers few, large, showy. Calyx of 5 sepals enclosed by 2 leaf-like bracts. Corolla white, 5-lobed, bell-shaped. Stamens 5. Pistil 1, with 2 stigmas. May-June.

Greek Valerian
Polemonium reptans L.

The name Valerian apparently is from the Latin word *valere,* strong, in allusion to the supposed medicinal properties of these plants. The name Polemonium is said to have been applied in honor of Polemon, king of Pontus. These plants are quite common in open woods throughout the State.—Stem about 1 foot long, weak and spreading. Leaves alternate, pinnately compound. Flowers several, in corymbs. Calyx of 5 sharp-pointed lobes. Corolla light blue, 5-lobed. Stamens 5. Pistil 1, with a 3-lobed style. April-May.

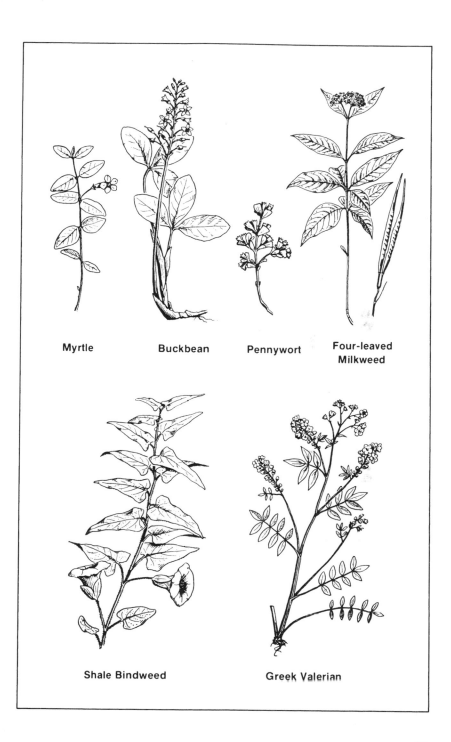

Myrtle   Buckbean   Pennywort   Four-leaved
                                                Milkweed

Shale Bindweed   Greek Valerian

Mountain Phlox
Phlox ovata L.

This attractive plant is distinguished from the other species of Phlox by the presence of short decumbent sterile shoots with persistent ovate leaves. It is found in West Virginia in woods in the mountain counties along the Virginia border.—Stem smooth, 1 to 2 feet high, ascending from a decumbent base. Leaves opposite, distinctly ovate. Flowers in flat-topped cymes. Calyx of 5 short, broad, acute teeth. Corolla pink or light red, with a long, slender tube and 5 rounded entire lobes. Stamens 5, attached to the tube of the corolla. Pistil 1, with a 3-lobed style. May-June.

Wild Blue Phlox
Phlox divaricata L.

These graceful, delicately tinted flowers are common in rocky woods in nearly all parts of West Virginia. The Wild Blue Phlox is one of the commonest and loveliest species of the genus to be found in this State.—Stem 9 to 18 inches high, spreading or ascending. Leaves opposite, oblong or lance-oblong. Flowers in a loose spreading cluster. Calyx with 5 slender teeth. Corolla pale lilac or bluish, salver-shaped, with a long tube and a 5-parted border. Stamens 5, attached to the corolla tube. Pistil 1, with a 3-lobed style. April-May.

Creeping Phlox
Phlox stolonifera Sims.

This species is quite similar to the wild blue phlox, but differs in having creeping runners from the base and reddish flowers. It is much less widely distributed and in West Virginia occurs mainly in the mountain counties, where it is locally found in rich woods in large patches.—Stem 4 to 10 inches high. Leaves oblong or ovate, roundish, obtuse. Flowers in close few-flowered cymes. Calyx with 5 long linear teeth. Corolla reddish-purple, the lobes rounded, usually entire. Stamens 5, attached to the corolla tube. Pistil 1, with a 3-lobed style. May-June.

Mosspink
Phlox subulata L.

Dry shaly or rocky mountain sides on the eastern slopes of the Alleghenies are clothed every spring with a glowing mantle of pink formed by the flowers of these little evergreen plants. They have been much planted in rock gardens and are quite successful. Although the common name seems to indicate it, they are not actually members of the pink family.—Stems creeping, forming broad mats. Leaves small, crowded, evergreen. Flowers in cymes. Calyx with 5 very slender teeth. Corolla bright purple-pink or sometimes white with a slender tube and 5 wedge-shaped lobes. Stamens 5, attached to the corolla-tube. Pistil 1, with 3-lobed style. April-September, the principal wave of blooming in April and May.

Swordleaf Phlox
Phlox buckleyi Wherry

This is the most remarkable of our West Virginia species of Phlox. It was first collected in 1838 by S. B. Buckley, probably at White Sulphur Springs, but lay unnoticed in his herbarium for many years and only received recognition as a species in 1930. Its entire range is limited to an area less than 100 miles in diameter, centering around Covington, Va. In West Virginia it is found only in Greenbrier and Pocahontas Counties, on shaly slopes in open woods.—Stem ascending, 6 to 20 inches high, mostly unbranched. Leaves linear, lanceolate or ovate. Flowers in compact sessile cymes. Calyx with 5 linear sharp pointed teeth. Corolla purple, pink or white, with a long slender tube and 5 obovate entire lobes. Stamens 5, attached on the tube of the corolla. Pistil 1, with a 3-lobed style. May-June.

Mountain Phlox

Wild Blue Phlox

Creeping Phlox

Mosspink

Swordleaf Phlox

Appendaged Waterleaf
Hydrophyllum appendiculatum Michx.

This species of waterleaf is easily recognized by the small strongly deflexed appendages borne between the calyx lobes. It occurs along with the other species in woods throughout West Virginia.—Stems 1 to 2 feet high, densely covered with sticky hairs. Leaves long-petioled, deeply 5-lobed, the lobes sharp-pointed. Flowers in loosely flowered cymes. Calyx 5-parted. Corolla 5-cleft, bell-shaped, violet or purple. Stamens 5. Pistil 1, with a 2-cleft style. May-June.

Large-leaved Waterleaf
Hydrophyllum macrophyllum Nutt.

The Large-leaved Waterleaf is found in rich woods throughout the State. It is easily separated from the other species of waterleaf by its pinnatifid or pinnately divided leaves, composed of 7-13 segments.—Stem about 1 foot high, densely hispid with white hairs. Leaves large, pinnately divided into several ovate, coarsely toothed segments. Flowers in dense globular clusters. Calyx 5-parted. Corolla 5-cleft, bell-shaped, white. Stamens 5. Pistil 1, with a 2-cleft style. May-June.

Pursh's Phacelia
Phacelia purshii Buckley

Pursh's Phacelia is easily recognized by the conspicuously fimbriate lobes of the corolla. It is found in moist woods or thickets throughout West Virginia. The word *Phacelia* is from the Greek word meaning a *cluster* and refers to the manner in which the flowers are grouped.—Stem erect or ascending, branched, 6 to 20 inches high. Leaves pinnately cleft, the lobes sharply toothed. Flowers in many-flowered clusters. Calyx 5-parted. Corolla 5-lobed, bell-shaped, light blue or white. Stamens 5. Pistil 1, with a 2-parted style. April-June.

Virginia Waterleaf
Hydrophyllum virginianum L.

In moist woods throughout the entire State the Virginia Waterleaf is a common sight. The name has no apparent meaning, since the leaves are not particularly succulent, nor do they form cups to catch water.—Stem 1 to 2 feet high. Leaves divided into 5 to 7 oblong toothed divisions. Flowers are 1-sided raceme-like clusters usually coiled from the apex when young. Calyx 5-parted. Corolla 5-cleft, bell-shaped, white or purplish. Stamens 5. Pistil 1, with a 2-cleft style. May-August.

Small-flowered Phacelia
Phacelia dubia (L.) Small

This plant is distinguished from the other species of *Phacelia* by having the corolla lobes entire instead of fimbriate and the appendages between the lobes inconspicuous or none. It occurs throughout the State in moist soil of shaded banks.—Stem 4 to 12 inches high, slender, spreading. Leaves pinnately cleft or divided. Flowers about ½ inch broad, in loose racemes. Calyx 5-parted. Corolla 5-lobed, bell-shaped, bluish-white. Stamens 5. Pistil 1, with a 2-parted style. April-June.

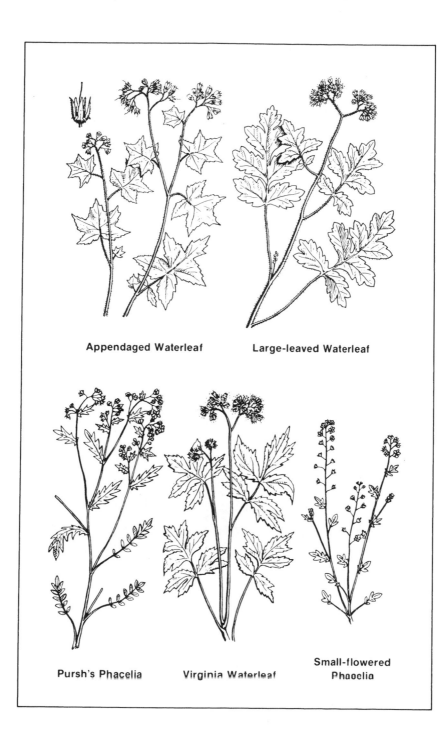

Appendaged Waterleaf   Large-leaved Waterleaf

Pursh's Phacelia   Virginia Waterleaf   Small-flowered Phacelia

77

Wild Comfrey
Cynoglossum virginianum L.

This coarse herb, found throughout West Virginia in open deciduous woods, is a close relative of the Garden Comfrey or Hound's Tongue. This plant is also known as Hound's Tongue, a name which refers to the rough leaves which are supposed to have some resemblance to the tongue of a dog. The 4-parted burs are familiar sights in late summer woods.—Stem 1 to 2½ feet high. Leaves rough, lance-oblong. Flowers rather few, about ½ inch broad, in racemes. Calyx 5-parted. Corolla funnel-form, with 5 pale blue rounded lobes. Stamens 5. Pistil 1, with a single style and a deeply 4-lobed ovary. April-May.

Forgetmenot
Myosotis virginica (L.) BSP.

On dry banks and in rocky woods, occasional throughout the State, we look for these exquisite little flowers throughout the spring and early summer. This species is a close relative of the garden forgetmenot, whose flowers, with the pale blue corolla and the yellow eye, figure in many stories and legends of love and affection.—Stem erect, bristly-hairy, branched from the base, 2 to 16 inches high. Leaves blunt, linear or oblong. Calyx 5-cleft. Corolla small. Stamens 5. Pistil 1. April-July.

Bluebells
Mertensia virginica (L.) Link.

These very lovely flowers are found in moist places, particularly in rich flood plains along streams, in most parts of West Virginia. The flowers are light pink in bud and change to violet-blue as they mature. In some regions the plant is called Virginia Cowslip.—Stem 1 to 2 feet high, smooth, erect. Leaves oblong, petioled, smooth. Flowers in clusters. Calyx 5-cleft. Corolla 1 inch long. Stamens 5. Pistil 1. March-May.

Corn Gromwell
Lithospermum arvense L.

This is a common introduced weed found in sandy fields, roadsides and waste places throughout the State. The name Gromwell means gray millet; the plant is quite common in "corn" (grain) fields of Europe. *Lithospermum* means *stone seed* and refers to the hard nutlets.—Stem 1 to 2½ feet high. Leaves lanceolate or linear. Flowers solitary in axils of the upper leaves. Calyx 5-parted. Corolla funnel-form, nearly white, 5-parted. Stamens 5. Pistil 1. May-September.

Sage
Salvia lyrata L.

In sandy woods and fields throughout the State the conspicuous flowers of the Wild Sage are frequently seen. The plant exhibits many of the familiar characteristics of the Mint family, to which it belongs, such as a square stem, opposite leaves, a two-lipped flower, and a deeply 4-parted ovary.—Stem 8 to 24 inches high, somewhat hairy, not much branched. Leaves nearly all basal, usually pinnatifid. Flowers showy, in a raceme. Calyx two-lipped, usually 3-cleft. Corolla 1 inch long, blue-purple, deeply two-lipped. Stamens 2. Pistil 1. May-June.

Hoary Puccoon
Lithospermum canescens (Michx.) Lehm.

The showy flowers of the Puccoon attract attention against the barren slopes of dry shaly mountain sides in eastern West Virginia. The plants are softly hairy and grayish-white (hoary) in color. The name puccoon was given by the American Indians, who used some species as a source of dyes.—Stem 8 to 20 inches high. Leaves oblong or ovate, downy. Flowers sessile, thickly clustered at the summit of the stem, the cluster curled up at the end and unrolling as the flowers open. Calyx 5-parted. Corolla handsome, deep orange-yellow, 5-lobed. Stamens 5. Pistil 1, with a single style and a deeply 4-parted ovary. April-May.

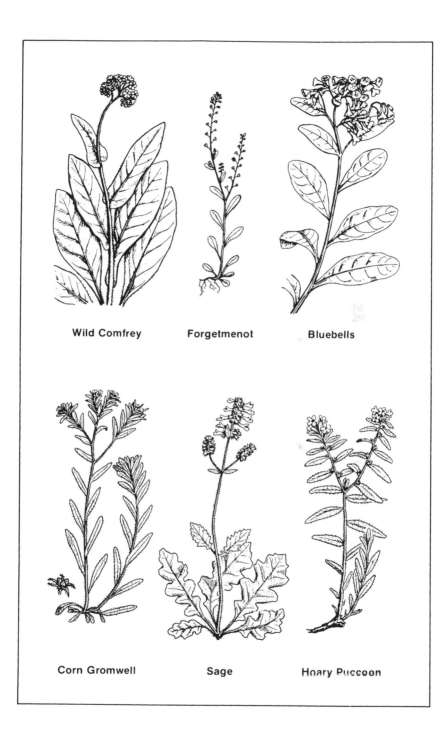

Wild Comfrey   Forgetmenot   Bluebells

Corn Gromwell   Sage   Hoary Puccoon

Groundivy
Nepeta hederaca (L.) Trevisan.

This little immigrant from Europe has made itself at home in a pleasant manner, brightening damp or shady rich soil near dwellings with a profusion of blossoms. It is a familiar plant in all parts of the State. It has the square stem, opposite leaves and distinctive aroma characteristic of most members of the Mint family.—Stem creeping upon the ground. Leaves kidney-shaped, crenate. Flowers loosely clustered in the axils of the leaves. Calyx 5-toothed. Corolla bluish-purple, 2-lipped. Stamens 4. Pistil 1. April-July.

Small Skullcap
Scutellaria leonardi Epling

This small branching species is common on shaly or sandy soil, particularly on shale barrens on the eastern slopes of the Alleghenies. The rhizomes bear tuberous thickenings with contractions between, somewhat like a string of beads.—Stem 4 to 12 inches high, pubescent, branched, spreading. Leaves sessile. Calyx 2-lipped. Corolla violet-blue, 2-lipped, less than ½ inch long. Stamens 4. Pistil 1. April-July.

Henbit
Lamium amplexicaule L.

This weed, an introduction from Europe, is common in cultivated ground and waste places, flourishing best in cool weather, dying down in the heat of midsummer and recovering in autumn to produce a late crop of seeds, in addition to those produced in early spring.—Stem low, weak, 6 to 18 inches high. Leaves rounded, crenate, the upper ones clasping the stem. Flowers small, in whorled clusters. Calyx tubular, 5-toothed. Corolla pale purple or magenta. Stamens 4. Pistil 1, with a 2-lobed style and a deeply 4-lobed ovary. April-October.

Showy Skullcap
Scutellaria serrata Andr.

This pretty plant is common in woods throughout West Virginia and is one of the handsomest of the 2 or 3 dozen American species of skullcaps. The nearly glabrous habit of this species separates it from its near relatives.—Stem 10 to 28 inches high. Leaves serrate, ovate. Flowers in loosely flowered racemes. Calyx bilabiate, bell-shaped in flower, closed in fruit. Corolla blue, 1 inch long, slender, two-lipped. Stamens 4. Pistil 1, with a deeply 4-parted ovary. May-June.

Hairy Skullcap
Scutellaria ovalifolia Pers.

The curious appendage of the calyx whereby it is closed as the fruits develop, gives the name to these plants. The word Scutellaria is from the Latin, *scutella,* a dish. The Hairy Skullcap grows in dry or sterile ground, quite common throughout the State.— Stem hairy, 8 to 28 inches high. Leaves crenate, oblong-ovate, blunt. Flowers irregular, in short racemes. Calyx bilabiate, bell-shaped in flower, closed in fruit. Corolla blue, ½ inch long. Stamens 4. Pistil 1. May-June.

Guyandotte Beauty
Synandra hispidula (Michx.) Baill.

This lovely flower, of the Lower Ohio Valley, although discovered in the late 18th century, has never had a common English name. It is abundant in rich woods in the Guyandotte Valley and elsewhere in the lower Ohio Valley, the habitats of the Wyandot (or Guyandotte) Indians, and the name Guyandotte Beauty is suggested.— Stem 1 to 2 feet tall. Leaves cordate-ovate. Flowers showy, 1 to 2 inches long. Calyx 4-cleft. Corolla yellowish-white. Stamens 4. May-June.

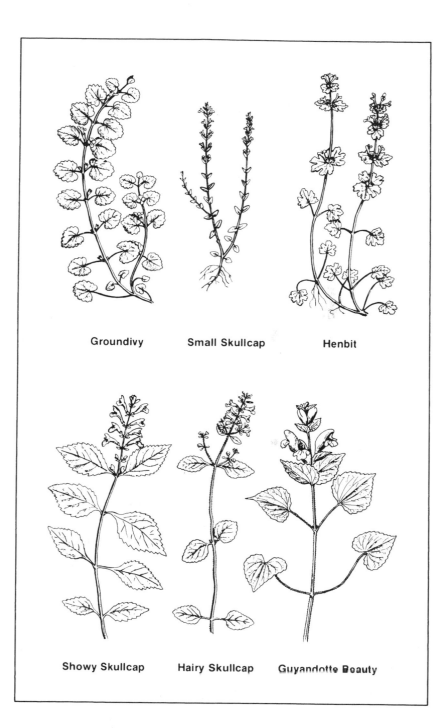

Groundivy   Small Skullcap   Henbit

Showy Skullcap   Hairy Skullcap   Guyandotte Beauty

Gray Beardtongue
Penstemon canescens Brittin

This is a common plant on rocky banks in most parts of the State. The flowers have 4 functional stamens and a fifth rudimentary one which does not produce pollen but is covered by hairs for about half its length, whence the name *beardtongue*.—Stem erect or decumbent, 1 to 2½ feet high, finely gray-pubescent. Leaves oblong or lanceolate. Flowers showy, in a slender open cluster. Calyx 5-parted. Corolla tubular, 2-lipped, 1 inch long, pale purplish or white. Stamens 4. Pistil 1. May-June.

Hairy Beardtongue
Penstemon hirsutus (L.) Willd.

The Hairy Beardtongue differs from the preceding species in having more spreading hairs, which are usually tipped with a knob-like gland on the end. It is found in the same habitats, rocky or dry banks, throughout the State.—Stem 1 to 3 feet high. Leaves oblong or lanceolate. Flowers in a slender open cluster. Calyx 5-parted. Corolla dull purple or white, tubular, slightly dilated, 2-lipped, the throat nearly closed by a bearded projection of the lower lip. Stamens 4. Pistil 1. May-July.

Common Speedwell
Veronica officinalis L.

The Speedwells are dedicated to St. Veronica, whose handkerchief, tradition says, was used by Jesus to wipe his face on the march to the cross and forever afterwards bore the image of the Master's face. This species, from its habit of creeping on the ground and rooting at the joints, is often known as Gypsyweed.—Stem hairy, prostrate and rooting. Leaves downy, toothed, oblong or elliptical. Flowers small, in clusters from the axils of the leaves. Calyx usually 4-parted. Corolla pale blue or lavender, usually 4-parted, the lower lobe smaller than the others. Stamens 2. Pistil 1, with a triangular ovary. May-August.

Thyme-leaved Speedwell
Veronica serpyllifolia L.

This is a common species which is both native and also introduced from Eurasia. It is found in damp grassy ground, quite common in all parts of West Virginia. The common name Speedwell refers to the transitory nature of the flowers, which drop very quickly.—Stem weak, slender, much-branched, 2 to 8 inches high. Leaves ovate or oblong, resembling those of the wild thyme *(Thymus serphyllum)*. Flowers small, in loose terminal clusters. Calyx 4-parted. Corolla 4-parted, whitish or pale blue with deeper colored stripes. Stamens 2. Pistil 1. May-July.

Corn Speedwell
Veronica arvensis L.

The Corn Speedwell, so-called from its habit of growing as a common weed in grain ("corn") fields of Europe, has been introduced into this country and has come to be abundant in fields and waste places in West Virginia.—Stem hairy, 2 to 15 inches high, often branched, at first erect, later reclining. Flowers very small. Calyx 4-parted. Corolla 4-parted, blue. Stamens 2. Pistil 1. March-September.

Neckweed. Purslane Speedwell
Veronica peregrina L.

This species is quite similar to the preceding, but is smooth or nearly so, whereas the Corn Speedwell is noticeably hairy. In addition, this species has long and narrow leaves, whereas the Corn Speedwell has short and broad leaves. The color of the flowers is another ready means of distinguishing them.—Stem 4 to 12 inches high. Leaves oblong, rather thickish (like purslane). Flowers very small. Calyx 4-parted. Corolla 4-parted, whitish. Stamens 2. Pistil 1. April-October.

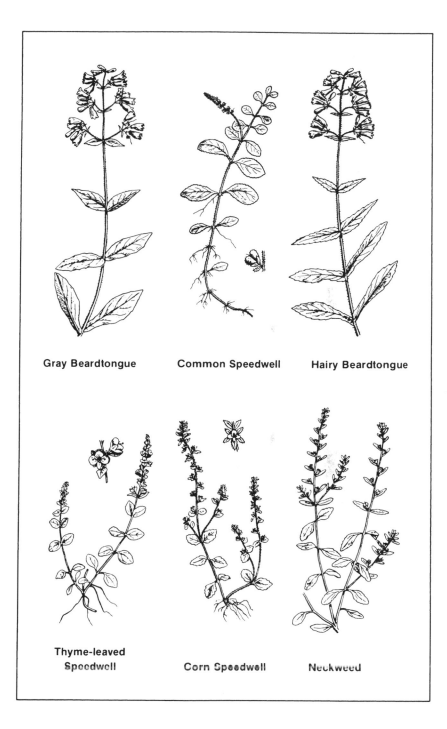

Gray Beardtongue   Common Speedwell   Hairy Beardtongue

Thyme-leaved
Speedwell   Corn Speedwell   Neckweed

Lousewort
Pedicularis canadensis L.

This plant received both its English and Latin names from the belief held by farmers of the Middle Ages that the presence of the European species in a field would cause their sheep to have lice. Though the idea was, of course, erroneous, the name has persisted. The present species is common in thickets and on shaded banks throughout West Virginia.—Stems clustered, hairy, 5 to 12 inches high. Leaves alternate, pinnately incised. Flowers in a short dense spike. Calyx split in front, oblique. Corolla dull greenish yellow and red, 2-lipped, the upper lip arched, the lower 3-lobed. Stamens 4. Pistil 1. May-June.

One-flowered Cancerroot
Orobanche uniflora L.

This is a pretty little plant which is totally parasitic on roots of other plants and has no green color of its own. The entire plant is brownish purplish or whitish in color. It is found in damp woodlands in all parts of the State, although usually nowhere abundant.—Scape naked, 2 to 8 inches high, 1-flowered. Leaves basal, brownish (not green) in color. Flower nearly 1 inch long. Calyx 5-cleft. Corolla pale lavender or purplish, tubular, curved, 5-lobed, fragrant. Stamens 4. Pistil 1. April-July.

Blue-eyed Mary
Collinsia verna Nutt.

These dainty flowers are, unfortunately, quite spotty in their distribution in West Virginia although often very abundant where they do occur. They are found in moist soil of woods and fields west of the mountains. The most striking feature is in the contrasting colors of the flowers, the upper lip being white and the lower lip blue.— Stem branching, slender, 6 to 20 inches high. Leaves opposite, the lower oval, the upper ovate-lanceolate. Flowers long-stalked, in clusters in the axils of the upper leaves. Calyx deeply 5-cleft. Corolla blue and white, deeply 2-lipped, the upper lip 2-cleft, the lower 3-cleft. Stamens 4. Pistil 1. April-June.

Indian Paintbrush. Scarlet Painted Cup
Castilleja coccinea L.

This peculiar species is a parasite on the roots of other plants, but is not completely dependent upon them, since it is green and makes a portion of its own food supply through photosynthesis. The upper leaves look as though their tips have been dipped into scarlet or vermilion paint. These are showy and are often mistaken for the flower, which is itself quite inconspicuous. The plants are common in low meadows and moist sandy soil in the mountainous part of the State.—Stem hairy, 6 to 12 inches high. Leaves alternate, entire or cut-lobed. Flowers small, in spikes. Calyx tubular, cleft down both sides. Corolla pale yellow, 2-lipped, the upper lip long and narrow, the lower short and 3-lobed. Stamens 4. Pistil 1. May-July.

Cowwheat
Melampyrum lineare Desr.

This little plant is found in dry thickets and on rocky heath barrens in the mountain counties. Although a native of America, it occurs also in Europe, where it is said to have been cultivated as food for cattle.—Stems up to 1½ feet tall. Leaves opposite. Flowers small, axillary. Calyx 4-cleft. Corolla 2-lipped, greenish-yellow. Stamens 4. Pistil 1. May-August.

Cancerroot
Conopholis americana (L.f.) Wallr.

This very peculiar plant, yellowish or brownish throughout, in appearance somewhat resembling a pine cone, grows among the decaying leaves, singly or in groups of several from a thickened base. It is frequent in most parts of the State, mainly in oak woods, growing as a parasite on roots of the trees.—Stem 4 to 10 inches high. Leaves non-green, reduced to mere fleshy scales which later become dry and hard. Flowers in a thick scaly spike. Calyx deeply cleft in front. Corolla brown or yellow, irregular, tubular, 2-lipped. Stamens 4. Pistil 1. May-June.

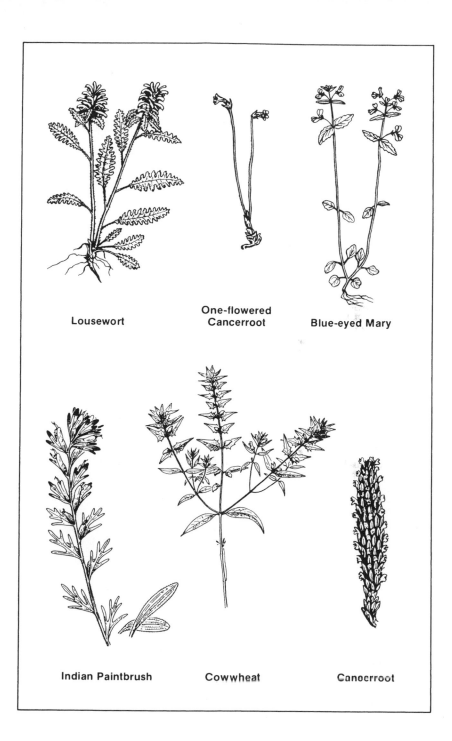

Lousewort

One-flowered
Cancerroot

Blue-eyed Mary

Indian Paintbrush

Cowwheat

Canocrroot

English Plantain. Buckhorn Plantain
Plantago lanceolata L.

This is another very common weed which has been introduced from Europe and is found in fields and waste places throughout West Virginia. This species is easily separated from the preceding one by its narrower leaves and shorter spike of flowers.—Scape 6 to 18 inches long. Leaves lanceolate, in a basal rosette. Calyx of 4 brownish sepals. Corolla 4-parted, greenish-brown. Stamens 4. Pistil 1. April-October.

Virginia Plantain
Plantago virginica L.

This densely hairy plantain is a native of America and is common in dry sandy soil throughout West Virginia. The flowers have a tendency to be imperfect and dioecious, that is, with staminate flowers on some plants and pistillate on others.—Scape hairy, 2 to 16 inches high. Leaves oblong or obovate, somewhat toothed. Corolla 4-parted, greenish-brown. Stamens 4. Pistil 1. March-July.

Broadleaf Plantain
Plantago rugelii Dene.

This is a very familiar and objectionable weed in lawns and waysides in all parts of the State. Many a boy has labored to remove these unsightly plants from grass plots and there is occasion for rejoicing that judicious use of modern weed destroying chemicals (2-4-D, weed-no-more, etc.) makes their eradication much easier.—Scapes 6 to 24 inches high. Leaves ovate, basal, in a rosette, the petioles crimson at base. Flowers small, inconspicuous, in a long, dense spike. Calyx of 4 sepals. Corolla 4-lobed, greenish-white. Stamens 4. Pistil 1. May-September.

Bluets
Houstonia caerulea L.

Roadsides and fields in most parts of the State are thickly carpeted with the dainty enamel-like blossoms of this little flower, often in such great numbers as to resemble a light snowfall. Harned says that among all the flowering plants of the Alleghenies one would have difficulty in selecting a more delicately tinted flower. Other common names are Quaker Ladies and Innocence.—Stem glabrous, erect, 2 to 8 inches high. Leaves small, opposite, oblong. Flowers small, solitary on the end of the peduncles. Calyx 4-lobed. Corolla 4-lobed, light blue, pale lilac or nearly white, with a yellowish eye. Stamens 4. Pistil 1. April-July.

Thyme-leaved Bluets
Houstonia serpyllifolia Michx.

This species, found in moist soil at high elevations in the Alleghenies, closely resembles the preceding but has its stems prostrate and creeping on the ground. The leaves are more orbicular and the flowers are somewhat larger and a deeper color.—Stems thread-like, creeping and rooting. Leaves small, orbicular or ovate. Flowers solitary on the ends of the peduncles. Calyx 4-lobed, persistent. Corolla 4-lobed, deep violet-blue. Stamens 4. Pistil 1, with 2 stigmas. May-July.

Cleavers. Goosegrass. Bedstraw
Galium aparine L.

This plant is very common in rich shady places throughout the entire State, although the small flowers are so inconspicuous as to cause it to be frequently overlooked. The name Cleavers refers to the manner in which the prickly burs cleave to clothing or the skins of animals, while the name Bedstraw was given because of the use of fragrant European species to fill bed mattresses.—Stems bristly, weak and reclining. Flowers very small, growing from the axils of the leaves. Calyx teeth none. Corolla regular, 4-lobed, white. Stamens 4. Pistil 1, with 2 styles. May-July.

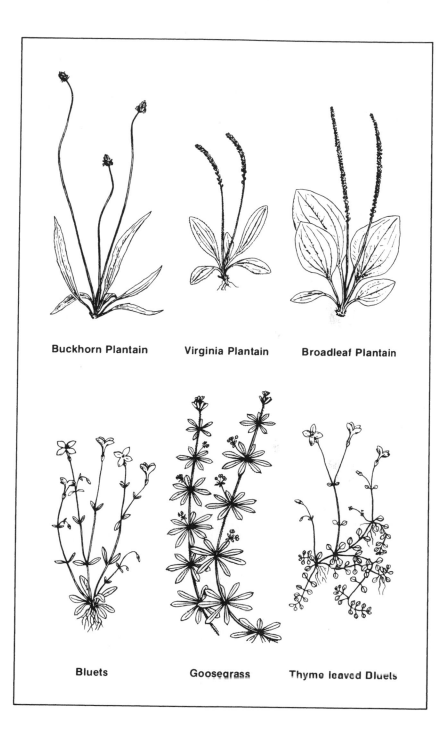

Buckhorn Plantain   Virginia Plantain   Broadleaf Plantain

Bluets   Goosegrass   Thyme leaved Bluets

87

Feverwort
Triosteum perfoliatum L.

This is a coarse hairy perennial that is common throughout the State on rich shady hillsides. The orange-colored fruits, ripe in August and September, attract more attention than the inconspicuous flowers. The common name refers to its supposed medicinal value. Other common names are Horse Gentian (i.e., a coarse gentian) and Tinker's Weed. It does not resemble a gentian, however.—Stem 2 to 4 feet high, densely sticky-pubescent. Leaves numerous, oval, opposite, with connate-clasping bases. Flowers sessile, solitary or clustered in the axils of the leaves. Calyx with 5 leaf-like, linear, persistent lobes. Corolla tubular, 5-lobed, purplish, yellowish or greenish. Stamens 5. Pistil 1, with a 3-celled ovary. May-June.

Rattlesnakeweed
Hieracium venosum L.

The purple-veined leaves of the Rattlesnakeweed, common in dry woods and open sandy places throughout the State, have a fancied resemblance to the markings of a rattlesnake and formerly were claimed to be a remedy for rattlesnake bites, another instance of the doctrine of signatures.—Stem (scape) 8 to 28 inches high, smooth, slender, naked or with 1 or 2 leaves. Leaves nearly entire, oblong, most of them in a flat rosette, usually conspicuously purple-veined or mottled. Flowers all strap-shaped, the heads clustered in a loose corymb. Calyx (pappus) of capillary bristles. Corolla yellow. Stamens 5. Pistil 1, with a 2-cleft style. May-September.

Dwarf Dandelion
Krigia virginica (L.) Willd.

The Dwarf Dandelion is a small species rather closely related to the true dandelion, but much smaller, the flowering stalks often becoming branched and leafy after the first flowers appear. It is common in dry soil.—Scape 1 foot or less high, later producing branches and leaves. Leaves roundish and entire or the later ones narrower and toothed. Flowers in small heads, all strap-shaped. Calyx (pappus) double, composed of chaffy scales and capillary bristles. Corolla deep orange-yellow. Stamens 5. Pistil 1, with a 2-cleft style. April-August.

Venus' Looking-glass
Specularia perfoliata (L.) A. DC.

Harned says, "In considering a plant which possesses such a classical name one might naturally expect to find in nature's mirror either a dazzling reflection of something quite beautiful, or at least a more striking representative of beauty than this very modest, simple, slender annual." The species is quite common in sterile open ground and grassy places throughout the State.—Stem 4 to 36 inches high, often leaning upon other plants for support. Leaves roundish, clasping by a heart-shaped base. Flowers sessile, solitary or clustered in the leaf axils, the earlier ones cleistogamous, only the upper, later ones producing a conspicuous corolla. Calyx 5-lobed. Corolla wheel-shaped, 5-lobed, blue or purple. Stamens 5. Pistil 1, with 3 stigmas. May-September.

Cynthia
Krigia amplexicaulis Nutt.

This species resembles the Dandelion, although it bears at least one leaf on the stem and normally produces one or more branches, each of which bears a dandelion-like flower head. It is found in sandy soil throughout the State.—Stem 4 to 24 inches high. Leaves mostly in a rosette at the base, toothed; those of the stem 1 to 3, entire, clasping. Flowers all strap-shaped in small heads. Calyx (pappus) double, the outer of chaffy scales, the inner of capillary bristles. Corolla yellow. Stamens 5. Pistil 1, with 2 stigmas. May-August.

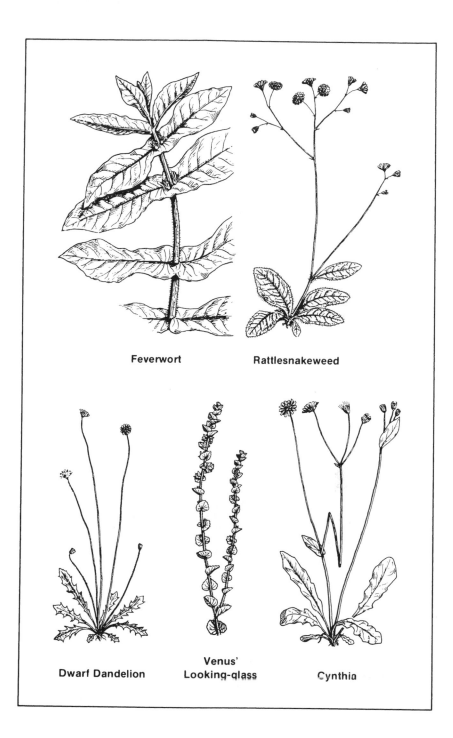

Feverwort   Rattlesnakeweed

Dwarf Dandelion
Venus'
Looking-glass   Cynthia

Common Dandelion
Taraxacum officinale Weber.

This common weed, perhaps the most familiar flowering plant in the State, is an introduction from Europe. The common name is a corruption of the French, *dent de lion* (lion's tooth), a name which probably refers to the jagged edges of the leaves. A name of similar significance is used in most European countries.—Scape slender, hollow. Leaves basal, pinnatifid or sharply incised. Flowers in large heads, (1½ to 2 inches across). Calyx (pappus) of capillary bristles. Corolla orange-yellow. Stamens 5. Pistil 1, style 2-cleft. They may be found in bloom every month in the year.

Red-seeded Dandelion
Taraxacum laevigatum (Willd.) DC.

This species resembles the common dandelion so closely that the two are often not distinguished when in bloom. However, the bright red-brown color of the ripe achenes contrasts sharply with the greenish or brownish achenes of the common dandelion. It occurs in dry fields and on rocks, probably in every county of the State, but apparently much less common than the preceding species. It is also an introduction from Europe.—Scape slender, hollow. Leaves basal, deeply incised or pinnatifid. Flowers in smaller heads (½ to 2½ inches across). Calyx (pappus) of capillary bristles. Stamens 5. Pistil 1, the style 2-cleft. April-June.

Plantainleaf Everlasting
Antennaria plantaginifolia (L.) Richards

Pussytoes is another appropriate name often given to this peculiar little spring flower, common in dry soil of hillsides and pastures in every county in the State. The flowers are of two kinds, staminate and pistillate, the former with disk-like creamy-white heads bearing dark brown, orange-tipped stamens, the latter appearing like white conical tassels.—Stem 4 to 20 inches high. Leaves obovate or lanceolate, the basal ones dull above, covered with white wool beneath. Flowers all tubular. Calyx (pappus) of capillary or thickened bristles. Corolla yellowish-white. Stamens 5. Pistil 1, with a 2-cleft style. April-June.

Early Goldenrod
Solidago harrisii Steele

Most goldenrods produce their flowers in late summer or fall and the extremely early appearance of this species separates it readily from the 24 other goldenrods of the State. It is found only on dry shaly mountain sides on the eastern slopes of the Alleghenies, and was named for Edward Harris, who first collected it at Cumberland, Maryland, in 1910.—Stem 2 to 3 feet high. Leaves ovate-lanceolate, serrate, rather thick and shining. Flowers in heads composed of both ray and disk flowers, these grouped in one-sided panicles. Calyx of capillary bristles. Corolla yellow. Stamens 5. Pistil 1, style 2-cleft. Late May-September.

Virginia Pussytoes
Antennaria virginica Stebbins

This interesting plant was discovered by Ledyard Stebbins in 1933 on the farm of Wilbert M. Frye at Hanging Rock in Hampshire County. It is set off from all other species of Pussytoes by the erose margins of the involucral bracts and the sparsely pubescent achenes. It is found in West Virginia only on dry shaly mountain sides on the eastern slopes of the Alleghenies.—Stem less than one foot high. Leaves tomentose, linear. Flowers corymbose, all tubular. Calyx (pappus) of capillary or thickened bristles. Corolla yellowish-white. Stamens 5. Pistil 1. April-June.

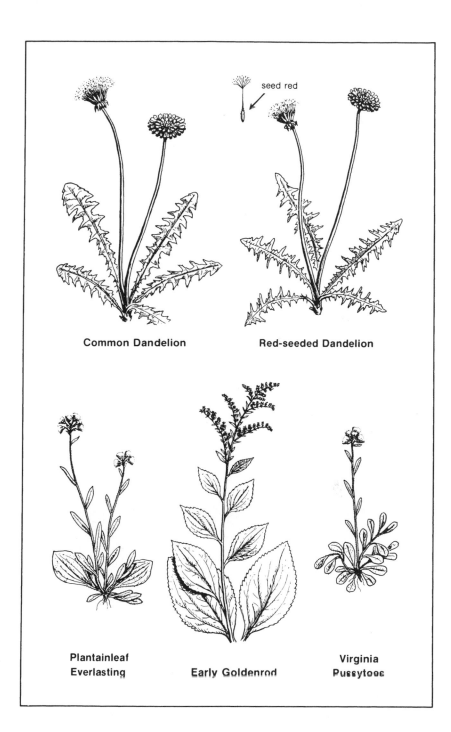

seed red

Common Dandelion

Red-seeded Dandelion

Plantainleaf
Everlasting

Early Goldenrod

Virginia
Pussytoes

Robin's Plantain
Erigeron pulchellus Michx.

This is one of the earliest flowering members of the Composite family, most of that great family appearing in the late summer or fall. It is found on shaded hills and banks throughout the State. The ray-flowers number about 50.—Stem 1 to 2 feet high, simple, hairy, producing offsets from the base. Leaves basal and cauline. Flower-heads rather large, composed of both strap-shaped and tubular flowers. Calyx (pappus) of capillary bristles. Corollas of strap-shaped (ray) flowers bluish-purple, of tubular (disk) flowers yellow. Stamens 5. Pistil 1, with a 2-parted style. April-June.

Coltsfoot
Tussilago farfara L.

The Coltsfoot, a native of Europe, has long been known in New England, but has spread across West Virginia chiefly since 1930, mostly in bare areas along highways. It is now one of the most familiar roadside plants in the State.—Scape a foot high when mature. Leaves appearing after the flowers, white-wooly beneath, conspicuous in summer. Flowers bright yellow, in heads somewhat resembling dandelions. March-April.

Philadelphia Fleabane
Erigeron philadelphicus L.

This is a very common plant, spreading by offsets from the base, found in moist fields and thin woods throughout the State. It is an attractive plant resembling Robin's Plantain, but can easily be distinguished by the number of ray-flowers, in this species ranging from 100 to 150.—Stem 1 to 3 feet high, slender, hairy, leafy. Leaves thin, oblong, clasping by a heart-shaped base. Flower-heads rather small (1 inch or less broad). Calyx (pappus) of capillary bristles. Corollas of ray-flowers rose-purple or pink, of disk-flowers yellow. Stamens 5. Pistil 1, with a 2-parted style. May-August.

Whitetop
Erigeron annuus (L.) pers.

During the late spring and summer, fields and roadsides throughout West Virginia are whitened with these very common flowers. The Fleabanes were so named from the belief that they would keep insects away, and for this purpose were formerly hung in farmhouses.—Stems 1 to 5 feet high, branched, hairy. Leaves coarsely and sharply toothed. Flower-heads small, clustered, composed of both ray and disk flowers. Calyx (pappus) double, the inner of capillary bristles, the outer of tiny scales. Corollas of ray flowers white, tinged with pink, of disk flowers yellow. Stamens 5. Pistil 1, with a 2-lobed style. May-November.

Goldenknees
Chrysogonum virginianum L.

The scientific and common names of this showy little plant are derived from two Greek words which refer to different parts of the plant, *golden* having reference to the color of the flowers, while *knee* refers to the joints of the stem. It is occasionally found in dry soil in most parts of the State.—Stem hairy, 2 to 14 inches high. Leaves opposite, ovate. Flower-heads solitary at the ends of long peduncles, composed of about 5 ray flowers and numerous disk flowers. Calyx (pappus) a small crown. Corollas yellow. Stamens 5. Pistil 1, with a 2-parted style. May-August.

Daisy Fleabane
Erigeron strigosus Muhl.

This species, also common in fields and along roadsides throughout West Virginia, somewhat resembles the preceding but can easily be distinguished by its entire leaves. Both species look like small daisies and in this State are often called Whitetop.—Stem rough-hairy, 1 to 3 feet high, much branched. Leaves lanceolate, entire or nearly so. Flower-heads in flat-topped panicles. Calyx (pappus) double, the inner of capillary bristles, the outer of small scales. Corollas of ray-flowers white, of disk flowers yellow. Stamens 5. Pistil 1, with a 2-lobed style. May-November.

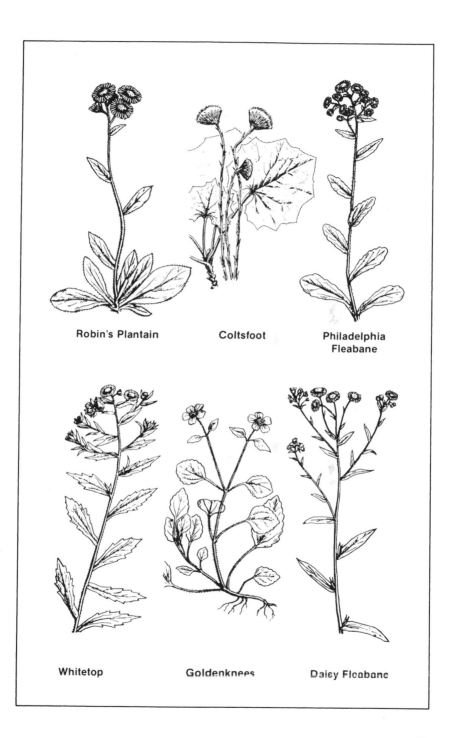

Robin's Plantain   Coltsfoot   Philadelphia
Fleabane

Whitetop   **Goldenknees**   **Daisy Fleabane**

Yarrow
Achillea millefolium L.

Yarrow is generally regarded as only an unattractive weed, but it has had a long and interesting history. According to legend, it was used by Achilles for healing the wounds of his soldiers at the siege of Troy, whence the name Achillea. In some form or other, it has been used, Dr. Harned says, for almost every human ill to which the race is heir.—Stem 1 to 2 feet high. Leaves deeply dissected, scented. Flowers in a flat-topped cluster. Corollas white. May-November.

Ox-eye Daisy
Chrysanthemum lencanthemum L.

Fields throughout West Virginia are brightened with this showy plant which is quite attractive to flower lovers but an obnoxious weed to farmers because of the difficulty in eradicating it from pasture land.—Stem erect, 1 to 3 feet high, simple or somewhat branched. Leaves alternate, toothed or pinnatifid. Flower-heads solitary or clustered. Calyx lobes (pappus) none. Corollas of ray flowers white, of disk-flowers yellow. Stamens 5. Pistil 1, with a 2-parted style. May-November.

Small's Ragwort
Senecio smallii Britton

This plant, named in honor of John Kunkel Small, a botanical explorer of the Appalachians, is common in meadows and thickets of the central and southern counties.—Stem 1 to 2 feet high. Leaves narrow. Flower-heads numerous. Calyx of capillary bristles. Corollas yellow in both ray and disk flowers. Stamens 5. Pistil 1. May-June.

Golden Ragwort
Senecio aureus L.

The flowers of the Golden Ragwort look like yellow daisies and are easy to identify, since they appear in the early spring when few members of the Composite family are in bloom. This species is found in wet meadows, moist thickets and swamps in most parts of the State, although commonest in the mountains.—Stem 1 to 2½ feet high, erect. Leaves basal and cauline, the former long-petioled, rounded, and deeply heart-shaped, the latter more or less pinnatifid. Flower-heads in flat-topped clusters, composed of both ray and disk-flowers. Calyx (pappus) of capillary bristles. Corollas yellow. Stamens 5. Pistil 1, with a 2-parted style. May-August.

Squawweed. Golden Ragwort
Senecio obovatus Muhl.

This species is quite common throughout West Virginia and rather closely resembles the preceding, from which it can easily be separated by the shape of the leaves, which are never heart-shaped in the present species. It occurs principally in moist woods and along streams.—Stem 1 to 2 feet high, erect. Leaves mostly basal, obovate or roundish. Flower-heads several, in a flat-topped cluster. Calyx of capillary bristles. Corollas yellow in both ray and disk flowers. Stamens 5. Pistil 1, with a 2-parted style. April-August.

Pussytoes Ragwort
Senecio antennariifolius Britton

This is another of the interesting group of plants endemic on shale-barrens of the eastern slopes of the Alleghenies. In West Virginia it has been found only in Hampshire, Hardy, Pendleton, Greenbrier and Monroe counties.—Stem erect, 12 to 16 inches high. Leaves mostly basal, oblong obovate, white-wooly, especially beneath. Flower-heads usually several, showy, less than 1 inch broad, composed of both ray and disk flowers. Calyx of capillary bristles. Corollas yellow. Stamens 5. Pistil 1, with a 2-parted style. April-June.

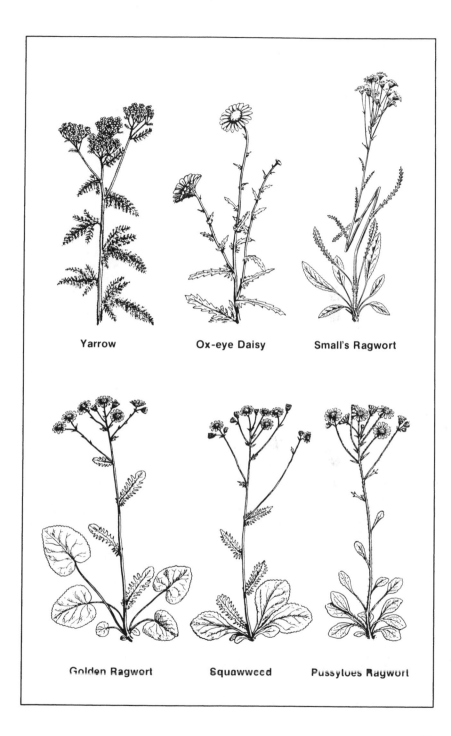

Yarrow   Ox-eye Daisy   Small's Ragwort

Golden Ragwort   Squawweed   Pussytoes Ragwort

Bibliography

For further information on the subject, students are referred to the following works:

FRANK H. BELL. 1945. The Genus Ranunculus in West Virginia. *Amer. Midl. Nat.* 34:735-743.

GAIL C. CORBETT. 1973. The Cruciferae of West Virginia. *Castanea* 38:214-229.

EARL L. CORE. 1966. *Vegetation of West Virginia.* McClain, Parsons, W. Va.

MRS. WILLIAM STARR DANA. 1919. *How to Know the Wild Flowers.* Scribner's, New York.

H. A. AND T. DAVIS. 1949. The Violets of West Virginia. *Castanea* 14:53-87.

M. L. FERNALD. 1950. *Gray's Manual of Botany,* 8th Edition. American Book Company.

H. A. GLEASON AND ARTHUR CRONQUIST. 1963. *Manual of Vascular Plants of Northeastern United States and Adjacent Canada.* Van Nostrand, Princeton, N.J.

WILLIAM N. GRAFTON AND CLAUDE MCGRAW. 1976. *The Vascular Flora of the New River Gorge, West Virginia.* Beckley, W. Va.

JOSEPH E. HARNED. 1936. *Wild Flowers of the Alleghenies.* Sincell, Oakland, Maryland.

HOMER D. HOUSE. 1934. *Wild Flowers.* MacMillan.

EUGENE E. HUTTON. 1962. Representatives of the Circumpolar Arctic Flora in West Virginia. *Wild Flower* 38:31-42.

ROBERT G. JOHNSON. 1969. A Taxonomic and Floristic Study of the Liliaceae and Allied Families in the Southeastern United States. Doctoral dissertation, West Virginia University.

THOMASINA A. REDD. 1969. The Ranunculaceae of West Virginia. Master's thesis, West Virginia University.

ELIZABETH STONESTREET. 1963. *Ranunculus ficaria* in West Virginia. *Castanea* 28:68.

P. D. STRAUSBAUGH AND EARL L. CORE. 1979. *Flora of West Virginia,* 2nd Edition. West Virginia University Press.

)

Index